Don't Try To Stop on a
Mountaintop

The Inspirational
Writings of
Robert Leslie Holmes

▲

Don't Try To Stop on a Mountaintop

EMERALD HOUSE

BELFAST  GREENVILLE
NOTHERN IRELAND   SOUTH CAROLINA

Don't Try To Stop on a Mountaintop!

Copyright © 1998 by Robert Leslie Holmes

Scripture references not otherwise identified are from the *King James Version.*

Published by

Emerald House Group, Inc.
1 Chick Springs Road, Suite 206
Greenville, SC 29609 USA
and

Ambassador Productions
16 Hillview Avenue
Belfast, Northern Ireland
BT5 6JR

www.emeraldhouse.com

Library of Congress Catalog-in-Publication Data
Holmes, Robert Leslie.
Don't Try to Stop on a Mountaintop
ISBN: 1-889893-25-0
1. Inspiration
2. Religion: Christianity
I. Title.

Mountains in composite cover photograph: I. Rozenbaum/F. Cirou

To
our children
Gary and **Catherine**
and
Erin and **Michael**
and to our grandchildren
Hannah and **Cameron**
who by their prayers and encouragement
are a special source of God's grace
and especially to
Barbara
this book is dedicated with love,
joy and thanksgiving.

Preface:

The Apostle Paul reminds us that special grace is given to make us see the wondrous mystery of God's love which He is pleased to make known in a variety of ways. Whenever God does communicate His love to us it is incumbent upon us to see ourselves as messengers of His grace, summoned to pass on what we have learned.

Because of this, it is my singular privilege to be a message boy for the King of Kings. In that capacity I have endeavored to deliver His message in these pages with faithfulness in order that others might be encouraged by it. If that happens I will have received my reward and my prayers in writing this book will be answered affirmatively.

Nobody writes a book like this alone. The seeds planted in an author's mind come from a multitude of sources and are germinated by God the Holy Spirit to bring forth His harvest. Very few of the thoughts in these pages wholly originated with me. They are the accumulation of years of reading, listening to and gleaning from the wisdom of others to whom I am indebted forever. Even the idea of writing them down was not mine first. It came by way of friends across the United States and beyond who repeatedly encouraged me to consider this exercise. I trust they will not be disappointed.

I am particularly indebted to my parents, the late Robert and Isobel Holmes each of whom was called home to heaven within the last eighteen months. From childhood they set out to introduce me to God and I know of no way to fully repay the debt I owe them. They knew this work was in progress before they died but neither of them lived long enough to see it in print. Paul's inspired pen tells us that what we see dimly in this life is fully revealed in that which is perfect. For that reason, I am confident my Mother and Father can see this finished book just the same. I trust they are pleased with the fruit of their labors.

My deepest gratitude goes also to all my teachers, formal and informal, lay and clergy, who from childhood until now have continued to reintroduce me to Him. This book belongs to all of you.

Particular thanks to Patricia Hetrick who carefully and patiently edited the original text and made helpful suggestions. Without her these words would have never been published. Betty Chapman, my assistant at First Presbyterian Church of Pittsburgh, demonstrated her usual patience with me throughout this project. My wife and special encourager Barbara was the first person to read the manuscript for each chapter. In every case she made wonderful suggestions that were almost always adopted. As you read these words imagine her fingerprints on every page for they are there, and I am grateful. To Pat, Betty and Barbara I owe a special debt of gratitude.

As children we were taught that parables are earthly stories with a heavenly meaning and that Jesus through His use of parables demonstrated He was the best story-teller of all time. Every parable within these pages is designed to point people towards Him. Some of the stories in these pages have been with me so long that I no longer recall when and where I first came across them. Nevertheless, I have searched my mind as far as possible so that proper credit could be given in the text. If I have unintentionally left someone out please accept my apology and be assured that where I am notified proper credit will be given in any future editions of this work.

Soli Deo Gloria

Robert Leslie Holmes
Pittsburgh, Pennsylvania
Fall 1997

Contents

One – Don't Try to Stop on a Mountaintop   11

Two – When Love Runs Late   21

Three – What to Do When Life Looks Bleak at Best   31

Four – Going Out With a Failure   45

Five – Demonstrated Love   58

Six – A Rabble With a Cause   68

Seven – Our Spiritual Nikes   80

Eight – Presbyterian Potatoes Are the Same   90

Nine – The Big Blessing of a Little Theology   99

Ten – A Bounteous Blindness   108

Eleven – When Success Gives Birth to Failure   116

Twelve – Not Hard to Make Happy   124

Thirteen – A Sure Foundation   132

Fourteen – Take God at His Word   138

Fifteen – The Things Christ Has in Mind   146

Sixteen – Christianity Lite   156

Seventeen – So Long Mediocrity! Hello Enthusiasm!   162

Don't Try to Stop on a Mountaintop

Peter said unto Jesus, Master, it is good for us
to be here: and let us make three tabernacles;
one for thee, and one for Moses, and one for Elias:
not knowing what he said.

–LUKE 9:33

A recent segment on television's *60 Minutes* news program warned about Internet abuse. Some people, it seems, feed vague, suggestive, false and often slanderous stories to the world wide web under the name of another. The result is forgery at a speed faster than ever before. In some cases otherwise highly regarded people and companies find their reputation and influence seriously damaged because of this. Inevitably, people who have no idea what the Internet is carrying in their name get blamed for misinformation they neither produced nor broadcast.

You can be sure that if the apostle Peter was alive today, he would never adopt these tactics. Peter was too short on diplomacy, and too long on candor, to try to hide behind some electronic pseudonym. People close to him never had to wonder what he was thinking. Peter usually blurted it out without much forethought. "Open mouth — insert foot!" That could have been Peter's motto!

Have you ever spoken in haste, only to wish later that you could take back your words? If you have, you probably sense a strange kinship with the Lord's favorite fisherman. One of the reasons so many Christians identify with Peter is that we have all spoken hastily at times. That Christ still loves quick-tongued people and makes a place for them in His plans, heartens us.

Irrepressible Peter got excited and said what he thought. Often some dumb sounding, impulsive statement exploded on his lips. This text is a case in point.

Peter said to Jesus, *"Master, it is good for us to be here: and let us make three tabernacles; one for thee, and one for Moses, and one for Elias."* Both Mark and Luke add a parenthetical, *"not knowing what he said."* They try to cover Peter's hasty notion after he witnessed Moses and Elijah talking to Jesus at the Transfiguration on Mount Hermon. It sounds almost as though these two gospel writers felt a bit embarrassed for poor Peter.

Only one week before, Peter's impulsive tongue landed him the biggest assignment Jesus made during His entire earthly sojourn. Having just asked the twelve who the people thought He was, the Lord turned the question in on the disciples: *"Whom say ye that I am?"*

Once again the big fisherman spoke without hesitation. The others might have thought through their answer, but not he: *"Simon Peter answered and said, Thou art the Christ, the Son of the living God."* This time Peter was right!

"Jesus answered and said unto him, Blessed art thou, Simon Barjona: for flesh and blood hath not revealed it unto thee, but my Father which is in heaven. And I say also unto thee, That thou art Peter, and upon this rock I will build my church; and the gates of hell shall not prevail against it" (Matthew 16:15-18).

Peter was as rough as the cliff face Christ had in mind when He changed his name from Simon, meaning Sandy, to Peter, meaning Rocky. However, Christ knew that with all his rough exterior, Peter had a well intentioned heart and Peter became Christ's first choice for building His church. That should be a word of encouragement for all of us who wish from time to time that we had better tongue control.

The days that followed Christ's affirmation of Peter's declaration were difficult ones for both of them. Jesus told the disciples that He must suffer, be falsely accused and crucified. Once again, Peter didn't like that and proceeded to reprimand his Master: *"Peter took him, and began to rebuke him, saying, Be it far from thee, Lord: this shall not be unto thee" (Matthew 16:22).* Such was the backdrop to Peter's mountaintop building proposal.

Such was the smell of impending death in the air, who could blame Peter for wanting to stay on the mountain with his Master for as long as possible? But, no one can stop with Christ on a mountaintop forever.

Building a Building Is Not Building a Church!

Fast talking Peter, recently commissioned as senior church builder, came up with a made to measure building plan. His would be a building of a type Christ never intended: *"Let us make three tabernacles; one for thee, and one for Moses, and one for Elias."* The Greek word may be translated either shelter or tabernacle. I suspect Peter had in mind to build a splendid three pronged church edifice.

Throughout the British Isles, where I grew up, many churches were originally constructed to commemorate some wonderful spiritual experience. Often further attempt to capture the moment is made by the church's name. Sometimes it is not. The same is true in Israel, the land of Peter and Jesus. Helena, the pious mother of the Roman emperor Constantine, traversed that land three centuries after Jesus and erected three architecturally splendid church edifices on sites her guide said were especially holy. Helena promoted building the Church of the Nativity marking the very spot where, according to her guide, Jesus was born in Bethlehem. She ordered the Church of the Holy Sepulcher built where she was informed the dead Christ was laid out long ago on the first Good Friday afternoon. Similarly, she had the Church of the Ascension erected on the Mount of Olives at the exact place her guide said Christ was last seen rising into heaven. There they stand in all their bygone glory, three great painted ladies begging for alms from all who pass by. Were it not for tourists and their dollars, those hallowed houses would be almost empty now.

A few years ago on a family trip, we visited another such building in the quaint English town of Salisbury, near Stonehenge. The once-packed, magnificent Salisbury Cathedral was originally erected to commemorate such a moment. It was an era when a movement of the Holy Spirit spread revival across England. Like wildfire, the Spirit brought men and women to their knees before Christ's cross. There, almost in the shadow of a pagan worship site, thousands once gathered to praise the true God of the universe.

Alas, no church building can capture even a split-second of spiritual power. Today, tragically, the Spirit's fire is largely quenched in England. A handful of dedicated workers struggle to keep the splendid Cathedral of Salisbury open. Had Peter built the finest tabernacle the world has ever seen on Mount Hermon it, too, would probably be an empty monument today. God's true glory refuses to be encased inside even the best stone walls. It is preserved ultimately in, *"An house not made with hands, eternal in the heavens" (2 Corinthians 5:1).* For *"house"* Paul uses the same Greek word Peter used earlier for *"tabernacle."*

Mountaintop Experiences Cannot Be Freeze Dried!

Peter wanted to stay there and begin his first building program. He coveted the joy of the presence of the big three, who together represented the Law, the Prophets, and God's forever Love. Who could blame him? Many of us would react the same way under similar circumstances.

Every Christian has "been there and done that." Some highlight spiritual moment touches our lives and we don't want it to end. It is entirely natural for us to feel this way. Nobody wants to go back to the real world when that happens. We all know Christians who spend much of their lives on a never ending quest for new spiritual thrills. Unfortunately, chasing after such spiritual rainbows, they are often among the most impractical people in the world, forever dreaming great schemes that never come to pass. Through them, no hungry are fed, no sick are healed, and the naked are not clothed. They have not learned, it seems, that we are not at our best perched at the summit. We are our best climbing against the odds in the name of Christ where the way is steep, and doing Christ's work in a world that does not always pause to say, "Thank you."

Maybe you don't equate your mountaintop with spiritual things, at least not in the usual biblical sense. For you it was a highlight moment such as the night you fell in love for the very first time. Maybe it was your wedding day, or the day your first child arrived. Few of us can forget the power of those moments and days. For some it might be the day a long sought after promotion was confirmed; for others, a graduation day when a hard won degree is conferred, or a new job is offered. Perhaps for others it comes with the achievement of hard-worked for financial or relational goals, or the purchase of a first home, or some other highlight moment. Perhaps it was release from a prolonged treatment for cancer and a declaration that we are cancer free. Whatever it was, or is, the message is the same: Don't stop there. Do not plan to stay at that point. Life has more to offer and the best is yet to be. Life is for growing. Had Peter stopped on the Mount of Transfiguration he would have missed Christ's resurrection and the experience God had in store for him on Pentecost.

And, of course, before that, Calvary. Little did Peter realize that the valley he was trying to avoid was the experience he needed most of all. It is the one we all need more than any other. In the betrayal and death of Jesus, Peter was confronted with himself as never before. There he came face to face with all his weaknesses and sins and was given a new opportunity to experience firsthand the grace of God in Jesus Christ. Whether we realize it or not, we all need to walk the Calvary road with Jesus. We all need to see ourselves for who we are and find the grace that sets us free to be what we are made to be.

Moments Versus Movements!

True success with God is not a destination, whether on a mountaintop or elsewhere. Life is not meant to be lived in still life picture perfect moments. It is intended to be a symphony of dramatic and exciting movements that come together to create a splendid epic that is better than anything

Hollywood has yet seen. True success is not a destination but the journey. Each mountaintop leads to a valley and the valleys are where we really learn to live and grow. Never be afraid of life's valleys. They are all a part of life's experiences that will be used, in due time, to prepare us for the new, exciting, as yet unexplored higher peaks that lie up ahead.

The Value of a Thorn

Christ does not call us to live on life's Mount Hermons. Mount Zion is our promised home. And we get there by way of Mount Calvary. Properly understood, mountaintop spiritual moments are good for us. *"Master, it is good for us to be here!"* But so are experiences in the valleys. In God's sight, one is as valuable to our growth process as the other. Peter did not yet realize that, delightful as mountaintop moments are, there are no peaks without valleys. For all their life-changing power mountaintops always lead to valleys. That is an inescapable fact of topography and of the Christian life. Peter's mountaintop was ultimately just a part of God's way of preparing him to walk the hard Calvary Road of everyday life in the service of Jesus. Ours are too.

The great old Scottish divine, George Matheson, is reported to have said, "My God, I have never thanked thee for my thorn. I have thanked thee a thousand times for my roses, but not once for my thorns. I have been looking forward to a world where I shall get compensation for my cross, but I have never thought of my cross as itself a present glory. Teach me the glory of my cross, teach me the value of my thorn."

In the same vein, we might also pray, "Lord, teach me the value of my mountaintops and the value of my valleys." Meanwhile, *"Pure religion and undefiled before God and the Father is this, To visit the fatherless and widows in their affliction, and to keep himself unspotted from the world (James 1:27).* The Christianity Jesus teaches calls us to feed His two-legged lambs,

17

who are hungry and need something to eat; thirsty and need a drink; strangers who need a welcome; naked seeking clothes; sick hoping for nursing; and prisoners lonely for a visitor.

Such an invitation may not sound so fanciful, nor even so romantic, as the mountaintop, but its rewards are far more blessed both to those who are faithful and to those whose lives they advance in Christ's name. His true call brings lows along with highs, suffering in partnership with pleasure, and work in alliance with highlight experiences. Our Mount Zion is a free gift. Christ paid its price in full on the cross; but we should never expect to travel home on a bargain priced ticket, for there is work to do in the meantime.

Don't try to stop on a mountaintop!

When Love Runs Late

When he had heard therefore that
he was sick, he abode two days still in the
same place where he was.

–JOHN 11:6

*I*n front of this sentence stands
a great affirmation that has something to say to our compulsive generation: *"Now Jesus loved Martha, and her sister, and Lazarus."* At the very heart and foundation of everything that enters our lives, however dismal or ominous it appears to be, stands the unchanging love of God's Son, the Lord of the cross, Jesus Christ. On a first reading, that may not seem like jump up and click your heels news, but it is, finally, the best news in any situation.

"For whom the Lord loveth he chasteneth, and scourgeth every son whom he receiveth" (Hebrews 12:6). Discipline is seldom fun. Sometimes it comes in the form of love that seems to run late. That is what happened here.

His Lingering Love Permits Pain

Our culture promotes pain avoidance. Dozens of advertisements tell us we can live without suffering. That is a myth because it is built upon a false hypothesis. The truth is that the best of medicines from the best of laboratories can bring only temporary relief. The fact that so many pain killers are on the market and under development ought to tell us that none of them works all the time. The Bible says that suffering is as normal a part of human existence as breathing. Job, Scripture's oldest book, describes life as being, *"of few days, and full of trouble" (Job 14:1).* Jesus promises, *"In the world ye shall have tribulation."* We would all be discouraged except that He adds, *"But be of good cheer; I have overcome the world" (John 16:33).*

Suffering deepens our dependence on Christ for strength and teaches us that He is worthy of our trust. J.I. Packer describes pain and suffering as, "God's chisel for sculpting our lives." The Bible never says our lives are to be pain free. Paul learned from his agitating thorn that Christ's strength is perfected in our weaknesses. Character is developed through suffering.

When God does not respond immediately to our cries in pain it is not because He does not love us, but precisely because He does love us. His delay is designed to accomplish some growing purpose in our lives. Mind you, I am all too aware that it is easier to say this when we are not conscious of any particularly painful experience in the present tense. While Lazarus was in good health, no one from his house came running all the way from Bethany to Jesus.

20

It was more than Lazarus and Paul who learned that deep pain is the way of strong growth. John Bunyan's name would be joined to theirs, as would the names of thousands of Christians in every generation. Bunyan's *Pilgrim's Progress* was written in the course of twelve years of suffering in Bedford Jail. Conditions there were primitive to say the least. The cells were small, cold, dark, and damp. The food was almost inedible. The guards were often cruel and the work was torturous. It is doubtful that John Bunyan would have requested one day of that captivity. It is more likely that he prayed for early release. Yet, had his prayers for freedom been granted immediately millions of us would have been denied a great Christian classic.

His Lingering Love Promotes Perseverance

The Old Testament scripture assures us, *"He heareth the prayer of the righteous" (Proverbs 15:29).* God is so determined that we should hear that promise it echoes in the New Testament: *"The effectual fervent prayer of a righteous man availeth much" (James 5:16).* He hears our prayers and acts, it assures us. Yet, it is important to remember that it never says instantaneous results are guaranteed. There is an old Irish proverb that says, "You get the chicken by allowing the egg to hatch, not by smashing it!"

"It's a waste of time to pray," she said. "I've been praying and nothing has happened!" We have all made prayers, and made them earnestly, but they were not answered. What happened to them? Where did they go?

Someone says, "You were praying for something that was not good." One of my predecessors at First Presbyterian Church of Pittsburgh, John Huffman, speaks movingly of his prayers for Suzanne, his daughter, after she was diagnosed with Hodgkin's Disease. People all around the world, including many in our Pittsburgh congregation, who remember Suzanne as a little girl, prayed for her healing. Would Suzanne Huffman's cure not have been a good thing? Of course, it would. Was it in the scope of God's ability to answer all those prayers with healing? Of course, it was. Yet, Suzanne died. It seems like such a loss when an intelligent, athletic, beautiful young person dies. When John said he lives now with a piece of himself missing, we all listened intently. Then he added that he knows where that piece is. It is in heaven, and one day all of John will be joined with all of Suzanne there. Then all of this life's mysteries will make sense. Meanwhile, John and Ann persevere with grace and with that pain that only parents whose child has died can understand. God's lingering love promotes perseverance.

Recently some members of our staff and congregation partnered to pray for me at the very hour I was scheduled to speak at that London Preaching Congress. I was deeply moved to hear about that kind of caring commitment in a trans-Atlantic telephone call. Then I realized that, because of a schedule change they did not know about, they had unwittingly gathered to pray one day early.

Someone later asked me, "What happened to those prayers?" Surely the answer must be that God holds them in trust for the very moment they were intended. Don't you imagine that somewhere among the vast bank of heaven's resources there is a repository for prayers once deposited to our account? Can you not imagine too, that those prayers will mature for payment at just the right time? Surely they include John and Ann Huffman's prayers along with the petitions of thousands upon thousands, no millions upon millions, of parents who pray for their children to be healed, or, to find the right partner, or choose the right path, or accomplish good for themselves and their world. Not for one second can I believe that a prayer is ever lost.

We have our first English Bible largely because of John Wycliffe. He was a persevering, praying man. His enemies, all good church people, determined they would do everything possible to ensure Wycliffe never finished translating the Bible into

English. Not only did those church people not cooperate, they persecuted John Wycliffe mercilessly. When he died, they burned his body at the stake and threw his ashes into the Thames. "We're rid of him," they thought. They were wrong. In God's providence, John Wycliffe's work was accomplished and millions read about God's love on Christ's cross in their own language because in the midst of adversity Wycliffe stayed with the job God gave him. His memorial in St. Paul's Cathedral, London, appropriately notes his impact on Christian history, aptly calling him, "The morning star of the Protestant Reformation."

Perseverance! When I taught college communication courses in Mississippi, a student brought this contribution to class about sticking to the goal:

Two frogs fell into a vat of cream
Or, so I've heard it told
The sides of the vat were shiny and steep
And the cream was deep and cold

"Oh, what's the use?" cried frog number one,
"'Tis fate, no help's around;
Goodbye, my friend! Goodbye sad world!"
And weeping still, he drowned.

But number two, of sterner stuff,
dog paddled in surprise;
And all the while he wiped his face,
and dried his creamy eyes.

"I'll swim a while, at least," he said;
Or, so I've heard he said.
It really wouldn't help the world if one more frog was dead!

An hour or two he kicked and swam;
Not once he stopped to mutter.
He kicked and swam and swam and kicked;
And hopped out via butter!

When we pray and it seems our prayers are not answered, it is not that God is not listening or that He is uncaring. We are not being ignored so much as challenged and grown. No praying breath, nor accompanying effort, is ever wasted. Job is right, *"He knoweth the way that I take: when he hath tried me, I shall come forth as gold" (Job 23:10).*

Join your hands with God's hand for the things you ask in prayer and be confident that the right answer will come in due time. His ear is not deaf. His arm is not short. And His love endures forever.

His Lingering Love Produces Posterity

To Mary and Martha, Jesus must, at least for that moment, have appeared neglectful. Surely when their brother died before them it looked as though Christ's love was running late. Yet, He never is lax. Even though, according to the text, no new messenger came to Him, the omniscient Christ knew what was going on. The whole situation was constantly in His purview. He was able to tell the disciples, *"Lazarus is dead" (John 11:14).*

This Christ who loved Lazarus, and loves us, never misses a sigh, nor a pain, nor a tear. He sees all.

It may seem as though our prayers are not being answered, but they are! He may not be working on our schedule, but He works always at the right pace for what is best. If what you want is good, hold fast to Jesus who said, *"Are not five sparrows sold for two farthings, and not one of them is forgotten....Fear not therefore: ye are of more value than many sparrows" (Luke 12:6f).*

When His answer comes it provides all we need.

Once I heard a song of sweetness,
As it cleft the morning air,
Sounding in its best completeness,

Like a tender pleading prayer.
And I sought to find the singer,
Whence the wondrous song was borne;
And I found a bird sore wounded,
Pinioned by a cruel thorn.

I have seen a soul in sadness,
While its wings with pain were furled,
Giving hope, and cheer, and gladness,
That should bless a weeping world.
And I know that a life of sweetness,
Was of pain and sorrow borne;
And a stricken soul was singing,
With its heart against a thorn!

We are told of cruel scourging,
Of a Savior bearing scorn,
And He died for our salvation,
With His brow against the thorn.
We are not above our Master.
Will we breathe a sweet refrain?
Then His grace will be sufficient,
When our heart is pierced with pain!"

(Anonymous)

Lazarus came forth! We shall too when it looks as though love is running late. Always remember this: We will rise again. Even death cannot keep us in the ground.

Look to Christ, Lord of Calvary's cross, Lord of every situation that ever has impacted, or will impact, your life. Believe Him. It is well, for He is Lord!

What to Do When Life Looks Bleak at Best

In the LORD put I my trust: how say ye to my soul,
Flee as a bird to your mountain? For, lo, the wicked bend
their bow, they make ready their arrow upon the string,
that they may privily shoot at the upright in heart.
If the foundations be destroyed, what can the righteous do?
The LORD is in his holy temple, the LORD'S throne is in
heaven: his eyes behold, his eyelids try, the children of men.
The LORD trieth the righteous: but the wicked and him
that loveth violence his soul hateth. Upon the wicked he
shall rain snares, fire and brimstone, and an horrible
tempest: this shall be the portion of their cup. For the
righteous LORD loveth righteousness; his countenance
doth behold the upright.

–PSALM 11

$\mathcal{D}$r. Delorese Ambrose, a visionary business consultant, teaches at Carnegie-Mellon University Business School. She also advises Fortune 500 corporations in transition. Recently, addressing a group of Pittsburgh business leaders about corporate re-engineering, Dr. Ambrose said, "If you are looking for security or loyalty in the workplace, they are simply not there anymore."

I don't like that. Yet, I fear it is true. Dr. Ambrose's message can be illustrated from almost any of the recent major business magazines. For many of us, phrases such as corporate downsizing and business re-engineering are really just polite metaphors for layoffs, cutbacks, and unemployment. Whether it is ABC and Mickey Mouse, CBS and Westinghouse, or some other uniting of names and initials, mega-mergers are the order of the day in corporate America. For many folk that translates into redundancy, salary reductions, loss of benefits, and, perhaps at best, relocation to an unfamiliar environment.

A dedicated professional directed a large West Coast television news operation for many years, often at significant personal sacrifice. A personnel file filled with commendations for good work and faithful service should have signaled security and appreciation for a job well done. Merger time came, and with it downsizing. He was laid off, allowed one hour to clean out his office, and escorted out of the building by security guards. He described it to me later as the most humiliating experience of his life.

Even more significant than the financial adjustments people are forced to make, corporate downsizing also takes its toll emotionally. It ushers in an era of uncertainty, concern about the future, or worse. *Business Week* was right when it termed the 1990s a decade of instability. People at every level of corporate life are learning the truth of that. The nineties have become the decade when some American business leaders demonstrated that dollars are more important than people in a way more blatant than we have ever seen before. The tragic true-life stories of that are seen all across our country.

Change is not always bad news, however. Some changes are necessary and good. Some make us better people. Some lift us to life on a new and unexpected plain. Friends who felt suddenly forced to relocate to a region they did not know did so with trepidation. This week they wrote telling us of their "splendid adventure" in a new place. What seemed a bad thing has turned out for their good. "While it was hard to leave so much that was familiar," they wrote, "we are glad now that we have had this opportunity to gain new insights and meet wonderful new friends."

In the Bible, Joseph had such an experience when his brothers sold him into Egyptian slavery. He soon learned that God is in the business of hiding serendipitous surprises in feared futures.

Sometimes change equals a threatening bleakness because we do not fully understand its purpose. If you are a person with responsibility for advising people about such changes you can help them cope with change by allowing them to know more of the big picture. It is probably impossible to over emphasize the importance of people in leadership communicating what the objectives of a change are to the people who follow them and who are most likely to be affected by their decisions. Informed people usually are less threatened by life's unexpected events.

Not Such a Bright Idea?

A cantankerous codger, stuck in the past, occasionally attended his old country church in a community without electric service. When the local newspaper reported that the power company was planning to run new lines through that district, a meeting was called to discuss what this change would mean for the congregation. Someone suggested it was an opportune time for the church to invest in a chandelier.

The old codger, true to form, expressed his opposition to anything new. Rising before the whole congregation, he began to state his case: "Don't even dare to think of such a thing," said he. "A chandelier will bring ruination to our church. There are three good reasons why I say so: First of all, if we buy one nobody will know how to spell it. Second, nobody knows how to play it. Third, and most important, when electricity comes we will need all the extra money we can lay our hands on to buy some nice lights!"

Some changes, despite their threat, are good. Some are not good. Some of us are right now coming to terms with news that demoralizes: The loss of a loved one, a threatening prognosis or a broken relationship.

Moral Change

On the moral front, it is the same story. Dr. Charles Robshaw recalled 1939, when a line from "Gone With the Wind" created a national stir. It was all because of Rhett's good-bye line telling Scarlett just how much he didn't care.

Contrast that with this: MTV is America's most watched television network for teenagers. Recently after MTV's president made a speech, someone asked him, "When it comes to moral standards, where will your network draw the line?" He smiled, "So far as we are concerned, there is no line."

That statement should set off an alarm in the head of every person who cares about America's young people, and about our future as a society. It forebodes a declining spiritual desolation. Current moral trends in our society will bring a bitter harvest to us all.

When sin is allowed to remain in a life it always ushers in bleakness. Sin is the most potent demoralizer known to humanity. I have seen good people caught up in its grips and

30

suffer from its soul-destroying ways. What went wrong, they wonder. What went wrong was that they drifted away from God, and from His Son, Jesus Christ. Sin's past produces guilt. Its presence in our lives decreases our sense of self-esteem. (Who can have a healthy sense of self living with an ongoing sin?) Sin's future promises only sadness and decay. Its best hope is bleakness in the life of all who harbor it, and in the lives of those they love.

A Brilliant Life Wasted

Lord Byron, following a life of perversion in the face of all his splendid contributions to the world of literature, said it best perhaps: "My days are in the yellow leaf; the bud, the flower, the fruit are gone. The worm, the canker, and the grief are mine alone."

Life, however, doesn't have to end that way. No life needs to continue in sin's trauma. Jesus Christ declares it is so. *"The thief cometh not, but for to steal, and to kill, and to destroy: I am come that they might have life, and that they might have it more abundantly" (John 10:10).*

If only the intellectually brilliant Byron had looked to God He would have found in Jesus One who died on the cross to take away our spiritual canker and grief. If only he had traded in the life he chose to live for the abundant life Jesus offers, how far different, and far better, his end would have been!

This is the real message of Psalm 11. You can know Christ's abundant life even in the face of oppression and uncertainty. You can look bleakness in the face and overcome its threat with victory. You can rise above its waves and ride them to safety. This is God's great plan for you when the future looks bleak at best.

If anybody knew about changing circumstances and discouragement David, the psalmist, did. As he penned the eleventh Psalm, David no doubt recalled how Saul recruited him to soothe the king's depression with music. Saul's children were quickly enamored with David's winsome ways. Saul's son and heir, Jonathan, made David his life's hero. Saul's daughter fell in love with David. They married. It was a fairy-tale royal marriage that brought rejoicing to all the citizens of Saul's kingdom.

Caught up in the excitement of the moment, the people gathered in the streets and sang songs of praise, *"Saul hath slain his thousands, and David his ten thousands" (1 Samuel 18:7).* Delight reigned all through the kingdom. In those days David's popularity was to Israel somewhat like what Princess Diana's popularity was to the people of the United Kingdom before her untimely death. He was the people's prince.

Alas, David's popularity went to Saul's head. The king, abdicating to paranoia, decided David must die. That is the setting in which Psalm 11 finds life.

Afraid for his life, David's well-intended friends offered him their counsel. They recommended to David that he run away: *"Flee as a bird to your mountain"* they told him.

By way of response to their advice, David wrote this song of faith. In so doing, he includes three sound rules for abundant living. Take them into your life and you can conquer any threat. Make them yours and life will always be better. I guarantee it!

Rule 1: Remember Where God Sits!

"The LORD is in his holy temple, the LORD'S throne is in heaven: his eyes behold, his eyelids try, the children of men."

Helen Keller, who spent much of her life in physical darkness, had an uncanny sense of spiritual sight. She said, "Keep your face to the sunshine and you'll never notice the shadows." Yet, the fact remains that it is not always easy to do that when life's traumas blind-side us. At such moments we lose sight of God's vantage point. We forget where God sits.

One of our astronauts, Jack Lousama, told of his view of earth from outer space. "With the naked eye," he reported, "we could see freeways, airports, and cities. We could see the green and brown patchwork of the farmer's fields and the beautifully painted deserts. When we were over Chicago, we could see most of the Hudson Bay and at the same time see our nation's capital city and Baltimore. We could see two-thirds of the way down the Mississippi River and out to Denver."

What is amazing about this splendid eye-witness report is its range; from the winding Mississippi to the Rockies' splendid peaks. Yet, that fabulous vista did not hamper the ability to zoom in on intricate details such as freeways and farmer's fields!

If ordinary human eyes can scan such a sight, imagine how much more splendid the view God's perfect eyes must see: *"His eyes behold, his eyelids try, the children of men."* That is to say, He sees us all. But, wait, there is more in a minute.

William Cowper gave us immortal hymns such as, "There is a fountain filled with blood," and "O for a closer walk with God." Still, for all his great talents, Cowper lived with manic depression's ebbs and flows.

One stormy night in desperation he determined, at wit's end, to drown himself. He ordered a horse-drawn cabby to carry him to London Bridge on the Thames. It was "pea-soup" rainy. After riding for two hours in that blinding rain, the cab came to a halt. The cabby acknowledged he was lost.

Bill Cowper, disgusted, decided to walk to the river. If the horse-drawn cab would not deliver him dry to his predetermined suicide spot, he would walk there in the rain. He left the cab and, within a few steps, recognized his own doorstep through the darkness. Blinded by rain, the cabby's horse had followed a circle.

William Cowper stepped indoors. Realizing that this God we know best in Jesus, *"observes the sons of men,"* and, more than that, controls the weather and the seemingly unguided pathway of a lost horse, Bill Cowper gave his circumstances to the Lord. He found strength for a new start. In that setting, he penned words that have carried Christians through trials ever since:

> *God moves in a mysterious way*
> *His wonders to perform;*
> *He plants His footsteps on the sea,*
> *And rides upon our storms.*

God is on His throne in the midst of every storm. He watches over our circumstances and guides the footsteps of every horse that carries us. No cloud covers us without His consent and no rain falls without doing good when we trust Him.

Rule 2: Remember Who God Sees:

"His eyes behold, his eyelids try, the children of men. The LORD trieth the righteous."

I said there is more. Here it is: God sees us all, but there are some in whom He takes a particular, individual interest. The original text is a splendidly human word picture.

Recently, in need of a new lens prescription, I discovered I could read better by removing my glasses. Details seemed more sharp when I squinted. Have you ever sharpened your focus by narrowing your eyes? Most likely you have.

The psalm's original Hebrew text says God does that for His children. Notice the subtle difference: The LORD *"observes"* everyone, but He *"examines"* the righteous. Some He observes through a telescope. His own He examines through a microscope. He cares enough to pay special attention to our details. Bill Cowper realized as never before that it is more than that God watches from a distance, but that God really cares enough to look especially close when trouble looms. God squinted through the rain, if you will. Bill Cowper knew that night that God loved him as though he was the only person God ever made.

In the same way also, God loves and cares for you. He is always looking out for you when trouble arises.

Is life getting on top of you? Does the future seem bleak at best? Take courage. Remember that God is keeping an eye on you. A new day looms just ahead, a day where only God has lived. For Bill Cowper it was a day for writing a hymn to inspire thousands, perhaps millions, of people for generations he would not meet but who meet him every time they sing his hymn.

Only God knows what it is He is planning for your new day. At the right time, you will discover it.

Rule 3: Remember What God Supports

"For the righteous LORD loveth righteousness."

Often God allows us to enter the crucible of discouragement so that we may find our real self in Him. Every trial is an opportunity for us to lean on Him and do the right thing in difficult circumstances.

As William Cowper recalled his experience in that rainy night of his soul he wrote more words that call God's gracious care to our remembrance:

> *Ye fearful saints fresh courage take;*
> *The clouds ye so much dread*
> *Are big with mercy, and shall fall*
> *In blessings on your head.*

> *Judge not the Lord by feeble sense,*
> *But trust Him for His grace;*
> *Behind each frowning providence*
> *He hides with smiling face.*

Dear child of God, your life's circumstances may appear to work against you. Your enemies may seek to run over you and crush you. But they will not succeed, for God loves justice. Negative forces cannot prevail. God always stands on the side of those who do the right thing.

Give thanks to God Almighty and take new hope in the Name of Christ Jesus who says, *"In the world ye shall have tribulation: but be of good cheer; I have overcome the world"* (John 16:33). There is a future far brighter than the best you have yet dreamed. God is already there, and He is looking out for you.

Always remember:

Where God Sits!
Who God Sees!
What God Supports!

Then, with your hand in His, move into the future confident, *"that he which hath begun a good work in you will perform it until the day of Jesus Christ"* (Philippians 1:6).

Going Out with a Failure

Peter remembered the word of Jesus, which said unto him, Before the cock crow, thou shalt deny me thrice. And he went out, and wept bitterly.

–MATTHEW 26:75

[Judas] cast down the pieces of silver in the temple, and departed, and went and hanged himself.

–MATTHEW 27:5

*P*eter, *"went out, and wept bitterly."* Judas *"went and hanged himself."* You will notice that Scripture records that each of them went out having failed miserably. Judas, the betrayer, seeing what his hypocritical kiss had bought, hanged himself. He realized that what he might do with thirty pieces of silver could never right his wrong. He chose to take his life. Peter, a betrayer of another kind, once bragged that Christ would not face death alone. Yet, when push came to shove, Peter denied he ever knew Him and walked away. It took a rooster's reveille to bring Peter to his senses. When that farmyard trumpet of the morn crowed, Peter realized how far he had drifted. He, too, went out, but he went out a different way from Judas. Judas's way led to death. Peter's way led to a new life.

There is no sense in me asking if you have ever failed, for I know already that you have. We have all failed, and, in the process, broken Christ's heart. *"All have sinned, and come short of the glory of God" (Romans 3:23),* says the apostle, leaving no room for exceptions. Earlier he said, in echo of the psalmist, *"There is none righteous, no, not one" (Romans 3:10).* We must conclude, therefore, that his inspired mind determined we are forced to confront our individual and inescapable culpability.

Even the Upright Are Downright Failures!

Where I come from they say, "If you've never made a mistake, you've never made anything." Painful words; but true. None was ever more right than the person who first said, "If you have never done anything wrong, you have never done anything right!" Making a mistake is first and finally only evidence that we tried to make something. Even perfect people buy pencils with erasers on the tip. Failure is the most common of all human experiences. There is no one who does not know it personally.

A Michigan bank president told Henry Ford's lawyer not to invest in automobiles because the horse was here to stay and the automobile was just a passing novelty. It was an error in judgment that cost his client a fortune. The great Gary Cooper turned down a chance to play Rhett Butler in *Gone with the Wind.* When Clark Gable accepted, Cooper laughed, "That picture is going to be the biggest flop in Hollywood history!" It was a mistake that made him the laughing-stock of Hollywood for a while.

When some of us count our failures they are more serious than these. Some of us have experienced defeat in our struggle for material goals and bowed to the temptation of crooked business deals. Our lofty ambitions did not produce what we expected. One wag said, "I got so tired of working on my first million that I set the idea aside and decided I would work on my second one."

Others, for whom temptation came too strong, know sexual failure. No failures dog us like those in the realm of the spirit. One of the most promising young preachers I know left the ministry and forfeited the calling he loved because of an adulterous relationship with a woman with whom he counseled. Today he drifts like a ship without an anchor.

Some must pick up the ragged threads of failure and start again after a divorce. We never plan to fail, but we all do.

As a pastor, I meet many people for whom the defeats and failures of youth still taste bitter. In dark minutes they find themselves thinking, "If only I could relive that day, I would do it differently." Yet, we know all too well that Omar Khayyam was right to record, "The moving finger writes; and having writ, moves on." No day once lived can be lived again, and one of life's wonders must surely be that so many of us come through adolescence so little scandalized.

Karen's was a secret shame, a sin of long ago that was over in minutes. Yet, she spent the best years of her life trying to forget, albeit unsuccessfully. She dreaded her dark moment ever being brought into the light. Her life was molded by fear of her sin sneaking out of the shadows. Physicians treated her for one ailment after another. Karen's real problem, however, was not in her growing list of symptoms. It was

39

in her heart. She demanded of herself a higher standard for forgiveness than God does. Having sinned, she could not forgive herself. It was for people like Karen that God's Son, Jesus, came to earth and died on the cross. Peter came to realize that. Knowing that Christ forgave him, Peter had no choice but to forgive himself. Judas never learned that lesson. Therein lies the difference between the two.

Two Lives in Contrast

The really big question in failure is not how we failed, no matter how serious it seems. The really big question is what did we learn out of failing? The day of failure cannot be relived, but, by God's grace, it may be redeemed. *"I will restore to you the years that the locust hath eaten"* the Lord says *(Joel 2:25).*

The primary texts before us are from the gospel story after Christ's betrayal: Peter, *"went out, and wept bitterly.* Judas, *"went and hanged himself."* They present two contrasting attitudes in the wake of failure. Peter, defeated by fear of being tied to Jesus, and Judas, defeated by ambition and greed, stand poles apart in Christian history. Everyone knows their names. Yet, nobody names a new-born Judas, for that name carries its own stigma. Yet, many a proud parent presenting a child for baptism says, "Call him, Peter." It's a strong name, a mark of honor. It means a rock and it always recalls the one Jesus loved enough to appoint him first lieutenant of His church, He Himself being always its Captain. It is the noble name of millions and has a place in every language where the gospel has been preached.

In Defense of Judas!

What is strange about that is that if I want to play devil's advocate, I can, at least on the surface, make as strong a defense for Judas' sin as I can for Peter's except at one point. Judas probably never intended for Jesus to die. Three years on the road with Christ had worn Judas' compulsive personality to a frazzle. He was tired. He was ambitious. He was impatient. He was frustrated. He reasoned that Jesus was taking control too slowly and needed nudging. With the right push Judas figured to force Christ's hand. If He would go ahead and declare Himself the Messiah Judas knew Him to be, God's kingdom would come. Evil would be history. Injustice would be a thing of memory alone. The thirty pieces of silver from the occupying, terrorizing forces was really just icing on top of it all. Judas, once a petty thief and later treasurer for Christ and His band of disciples, knew the need for money. All his life he could never get enough of it. How can we know for sure Judas did not secretly intend to add it to the sacred treasury of the twelve when Christ came to His rightful office? What would be so wrong with that?

Have you never been tired? Impatient? Compulsive? Frustrated? Angry beyond control? Have you ever said or done something you wished later you had not done, or done differently? You know you have. All of us have spoken and acted in haste.

Following through with this line of defense, I would point out that Peter, on the other hand, was a coward and a braggart. He was all talk. After pledging to stick by Jesus, when the going got tough, Peter kept his distance. Challenged, he said he was not one of the Lord's disciples. Still, give him a second chance. Sure enough, given a second chance, Peter disowned Him again. This time he backed up his denial of Jesus with an oath. Give him a third chance. After all, he said he is not the kind of fellow to desert his friends. Perhaps, having had two opportunities to reflect on his earlier responses, he will answer better this time. If, as some say, the third time is a charm, for Peter it was a curse. Once again the rock crumbled. He lied once more, this time with a volley of swear words. Three strikes and you are out, Peter!

In our society, we put three time losers in jail for life without parole.

No Defense!

Alas, however, I am forced to acknowledge that what was wrong was not so much what happened that last night, as what had not happened before that night came. What was really wrong was that Judas had not entered a life-changing relationship with Jesus. Thus, he was left defenseless. He lacked a vital relationship with the Lord. Like millions before and since, Judas never came all the way to Jesus and so was running in the old ruts of trying to work things out his own way. Judas fell. So did Peter. Yet, Peter got up again.

The Judas Germ

So, why do we love Peter and hate Judas? I suspect the reason we hate Judas is that we see too much of ourselves in him. We all have the Judas virus lurking inside us waiting for a moment of weakness that it might attack us unexpectedly. We don't like to admit that perhaps. Yet, there it is. Some of us sold Jesus out yesterday. Others, thinking we were under cover of darkness, sold Him out last night, or one night when we were young. Some of us, perhaps unwittingly, are already planning to sell Him out in our next business deal. If truth be known, we would sell Christ out for much less than thirty pieces of silver would buy in the Graeco-Roman world of Judas' day!

In the book *The Day America Told the Truth*, a question was asked of hundreds of people all across our country: "What would you be willing to do for $10 million?" A whopping 25% answered they would abandon their family. The same number said they would abandon their church and religion.

Almost that many, 23%, said they would be willing to prostitute their body for one week. Seven percent replied they would be willing to kill a stranger. When I read those numbers I thought they had to be wrong. I was comforted by the knowledge that I spend most of my life around church people and they place a high value on things like family, church, self-esteem, and concern for other people. Or, do they? All of a sudden, I remembered instances from my pastoral ministry of some twenty-five years when I dealt with church members who have done all those things for a lot less than $10 million. When it comes to temptation and falling into sin, none of us is immune. The church, you see, is not a haven for saints. It is a hospital for sinners. Left to our own devices, there are no limits to how far we might drift away from Christ.

How to Fly Again Following a Failure

Here is the difference: Peter *"went out, and wept."* Judas *"went and hanged himself."* Peter confronted his failure and wept the tears of repentance. By the Lord's renewing grace, he found a fourth chance and he seized it with all the might he could find in Christ's Holy Spirit. He got up again. He rose above his failure. He invested his life in serving the Lord he thrice denied. Judas, on the other hand, faced with his failure, further took matters into his own hands. Therein lies the gospel's practical heart.

Failure is never final, until you determine not to try again. It does not matter if you are a three times loser or a three-hundred times loser. Do not worry about failure so much as about the times you did not even try. And always remember this: There is a way back to God. When you lock horns with your failure, that is, when you look it square in the eye with no denial and no excuse, Jesus always meets you where you are with another chance. He met Peter back by the boat ramp and called him to follow again.

God has a splendid way of using those who know defeat when they admit their failure. The Bible is a perfect textbook of practical examples.

I am thinking about con man Jacob, whose very name means, "A deceiver." In the Lord's hands, Jacob received a new name, "Israel," meaning "God's prince." God made the cheater a man of honor among His people. What a name! What a gracious God!

God took adulterer and murderer, David, and made him into a favorite songwriter for thousands of years to come. He penned more psalms than anyone else.

In the Lord's hands, Mary Magdalene, once a harlot, was transformed into a wonderful heroine for men and women alike.

Saul of Tarsus, the murderous fanatic, God transformed into the great apostle of the gentiles and the father of world missions.

In redeeming power, the Lord chose the sexually perverted Augustine and raised him up to become the great theologian and revivalist of the Reformed faith.

The playboy and maniacally depressed Francis of Assisi, God remade as the saintly jovial monk his fellow monks lovingly nick-named, "Jocular Domini," or "the Lord's prankster."

The testimonies of thousands upon thousands of saints who were not always saintly, in every generation for almost two millennia, bear witness to the gospel's ability to radically reconstruct lives.

Nearer to our generation there is R.H. Macy, who failed in business seven times before his New York store finally caught on. Suppose he had quit after the sixth downfall? Instead, Macy allowed each experience of failure to be his school to teach him what to do better next time around. Drunk with power, Chuck Colson was Richard Nixon's, "hatchet man." Someone said he would run over his own granny to advance

Nixon's cause. After Watergate, Colson turned to Christ. He learned that every failure is redeemed in Him.

Weight or Wings? We Decide!

When Jesus Christ comes to someone who has failed, He always brings a choice of weight or wings. Our failures can weigh us down or, redeemed in grace, can be the wings on which we rise to become newer, wiser disciples. The choice of weight or wings is ours to make. Christ's hope is we will choose wings over weight for he already took the weight of all our failures upon Himself on the cross. When He comes to us again there is no telling what He has in mind, but it is always that which is highest and best for us. Why, then, is it that so many resist Him?

Perhaps, through these words, God is coming to you as you struggle in the aftermath of failure. The promise His word makes is that when we admit our failures before His Son, Jesus, there will always be another chance.

Judas, unlike Peter, let his sin become his master. Once again he took things into his own hands. This time it led him to suicide. Someone called suicide "ending it all." That is a terrible misnomer. To commit suicide because of some failure, is to go out into eternity with unresolved sin still attached to your memory. It misses God's gracious forgiveness and leaves those who love us most with a memory that is hard to heal. We are not told whether Judas left a family but we know for certain that, because he took his own life, he left a record of unresolved sin. In the eyes of the world, Judas stands damned for all time. Judas never experienced the forgiveness Christ would have extended to him if only he had acknowledged his failure asked for grace. Thirty pieces of silver could not right his wrong, but Christ through the redeeming blood of Calvary could have done it, and would. Had he confessed his sin, Judas would have found that Christ is always more ready to forgive than we are to ask Him.

When failure knocks at your life's door, Peter's way and Judas's way are still options. In the face of our failures, which one will we take? Choose Peter's way. It is the way of Jesus who loved us all the way to Calvary and loves us still.

Demonstrated Love

God commendeth his love toward us, in that,
while we were yet sinners, Christ died for us.

−ROMANS 5:8

*I*t is a true story: When Warden Lewis Lawes came to Sing Sing in 1920, he inherited the most despicable place on this continent. Warden Lawes immediately introduced reforms that treated the prisoners like people instead of things. The inmates noticed the difference right away. When they expressed gratitude, Lawes directed the credit to his wife, Kathryn. Kathryn Lawes was a disciple of Jesus and believed Christ's redemption could transform any life.

Sometimes Kathryn took her three children to visit inmates who had no visitors. They were rapists, murderers, and some of the most notorious gangsters in American history. In spite of that, she never showed fear. She encouraged prisoners known to be undergoing a particular difficulty by extending a personal touch in some thoughtful way.

In 1937, seventeen years after the Lawes arrived at Sing Sing, a car accident took Kathryn Lawes' life. The next day her casket lay in the Warden's house a quarter mile from the prison compound. At exercise time the deputy warden noticed the prisoners were not gathering in groups or playing basketball, as they usually did. Instead, they gathered silently around the fence that faced the home. Some of the men looked as though they were praying. He knew what they were thinking.

Leaving his station, the deputy warden stepped before the prisoners and said, "Men, I'm going to trust you. You can go to the house." He ordered the main gate opened and the men walked out. No count was taken. No roll was called. No guards were dispatched. That evening at countdown, not one man was missing! Love for one who demonstrated love for them, made murderers, rapists, and gangsters people to be trusted.

Such is the amazing hope God has for us in the gospel: *"God commendeth his love toward us, in that, while we were yet sinners, Christ died for us."* Paul's declaration brings us face to face with Calvary's cross as the masterwork of God's redeeming love.

Good Questions!

There are some things that cause reasonable people to question God's love. Where, for example, is a loving God when little children starve in Biafra?

Where was God when an airplane barrels into the ground near an airport with a loss of hundreds of lives?

How was God's love demonstrated when an Amish baby died at Children's Hospital a couple of months ago, leaving behind a broken-hearted family?

Or, when a fifteen year old was shot by another fifteen year old for no apparent reason in a Homewood ghetto on Pittsburgh's Eastside?

Or, when a young minister was murdered on the Eastside while he was coming home from a Bible study at Carnegie-Mellon University?

Where was God when a six year old Colorado beauty queen was molested and strangled in her own home the day after Christmas?

Where was this love of God when the life of a bright forty-one year old business executive with so much to offer was cut off suddenly and without warning in front of his children?

Children and rational people dare to ask such questions, and who would blame them?

The Answer!

"God commendeth his love toward us, in that, while we were yet sinners, Christ died for us." Daily reports in hometown newspapers and on television in every major American city seem to speak against this truth we all want to trust, yet the death of God's Son on Calvary's cross overshadows them all. In that we find the nearest thing to an answer available for now.

I do not mean to imply that because of Christ's death our tears are dried away instantly; or that problems disappear into thin air because we believe what Paul writes here.

The truth is that non-Christians and Christians alike seek answers to these questions, and no one really knows. The darkness of loss blinds us all, and in its own strange way, makes us one. But we who trust Christ are more readily satisfied to know our questions will find their answers in the morning of eternal brightness that Christ procured for us on

His cross. There are circumstances and situations for which none of us have perfect answers, and anyone who tells you they do is not playing straight with you.

We Have Hope!

What we do have is hope. As believers, we believe the answer is on its way. In the meantime, *"We see through a glass, darkly; but then face to face" (1 Corinthians 13:12)*. All we have to rely upon until then is that God does love us, and the proof of that love is the death of God's Son for us.

Do not miss this love's everyday nature. It is not a past tense love Paul speaks of. He does not write that love was demonstrated on Calvary. There is a perpetual present to it. God *"demonstrates,"* says the apostle. Some Bible statements are historical. They happened once, achieved their purpose and were put away, as it were. *"The LORD shut [Noah] in [the ark]" (Genesis 7:16)*. That happened one time a long time ago. Meanwhile, knowledge grows, thoughts develop and theories change. A lot of water flows over the dam in the meantime. Yet one fact about God stands unmoved every day. At the core of all things, unshaken and unshakable, is Calvary love.

God's love for us is more than a Good Friday afternoon romance. It is the most alive love story ever. In each generation, it transforms people who do bad things into children of God. It gives those with no respect, self-respect, and those with no life, life eternal. It says that no matter what others think about us, Christ favors us before Himself. To those the world deems worthless it says He values you in terms all the wealth in the world cannot equal. God loves you today, and that is a fact.

There are many kinds of love. One builds up, exalts, and seeks the best for its beloved, while another drags its beloved down to its own level. One love is nothing but lust disguised, while another dreams the best for its beloved, and does all it can to help make the best things happen.

The love of God is greater by far than the best of human love. His love is a love with no limits that deems no price too great to pay. It is a love so all sufficient it leaves nothing for us to do but believe it with all our heart. Isn't that amazing! There are no conditions to the way God loves us. All we must do to know His love is trust Him for it.

The Love of God on Calvary's Cross!

Turn your focus to Calvary's cross. In your mind's eye see the scene there. Who was that between two thieves with pierced hands and feet, but God's only Son. No patriot ever loved like that. Nor did any mother, though a healthy mother love must surely be the nearest thing we can know to it. No human love can ever compare to Christ Jesus hanging in shame before a mocking mob. His love that day was, and still is, wide enough to embrace every person ever born; and long enough to go with us however far we wander. It was deep enough to stretch down into hell; and high enough to raise us to all God dreams for us.

A New England couple were engaged only a few weeks when America got involved in the Second World War. Wedding plans were postponed by the country's call. At the station, as he boarded the train that would take him towards basic training, they pledged to write daily letters to each other, which they did. As each letter arrived, she read it and dreamed of the day he would come back from the war.

Then, without warning, the mail box was empty. His letters stopped coming. "I'll get one tomorrow," she thought. She did not. Weeks went by and no letters came. Taking his letters from the drawer where she saved them like precious treasure, she untied the ribbon that held them together. She read and re-read each one. It was not the same as getting a

51

new letter every day, but it was something to hold to as she continued to hope that a new letter might come soon.

Finally, one day a letter did come. His name, rank, and number was on the envelope, but the writing was different. She ripped the envelope apart and found one sheet inside. One sheet!

One sheet that ripped away her dreams.

He wrote, "Something has happened and I have terrible news for you. I was severely wounded in battle and have lost both my arms. Someone else writes this for me. I love you as much as ever, but feel I must release you from the obligation of our engagement. Move on with your life. You will be better without me."

Tears rolled off her cheeks and blotched the ink as she read his letter again. She took pen and paper in hand, but could find no words to answer. It was too hard. She decided not to write back.

Instead, at the station where not long before they kissed goodbye, she boarded a train for New York. She rushed to the docks where huge vessels prepared to cross the Atlantic. Taking her hard earned dollars from her pocket, she purchased a ticket on a ship headed for Europe. In a strange land she found her way to the military hospital listed on that envelope. Tearfully, she searched among the wounded and dying for the man who had given her his ring. When she found him, she threw her arms around his neck, kissed him, and said, "From this day forward, my arms are your arms, just as my heart is yours. I will take care of you always. There is nothing that we cannot do together."

Christ has no arms but our arms with which to embrace our generation and our world. He has no heart but our heart to love the lost, and the lonely, and the broken, and the wounded. If there is one thing more wonderful than this love of God we receive every day it must surely be that He invites us to pass it on in His name.

At First Presbyterian Church of Pittsburgh one of my favorite lines in our congregational Mission Statement says, "Our highest priority is to proclaim Christ's cross and resurrection and demonstrate His love." Our mission is to make that more than a noble, high sounding sentence by putting shoe leather on it. This is a worthy goal for all who follow Jesus. As we link arms and hearts with Christians all across America and around the world there is nothing we cannot do together.

May such grace be given to all who love our Lord Jesus, and are loved every day by Him whose love runs all the way to Calvary.

A Rabble with a Cause

The chief priests moved the people, that he should rather release Barabbas unto them.

−MARK 15:11

*I*t was over one hundred years ago, but in Boston the memories still linger. It was the spring of 1894, and the Baltimore Orioles traveled to Boston to play what everyone expected would be a routine baseball game. Yet, what happened that spring day was anything but routine.

As fans on each side cheered for their team to win, Orioles' team member, John McGraw, got into a fight with Boston's third baseman. Afterwards nobody could remember what the conflict started over, which is a statement about how relatively unimportant it must have been. What we remember one hundred years later is that less than one minute later every player on both teams joined in a real donnybrook of a brawl. What had been one player against a member of the opposing team became team against team with no holds barred.

The fighting of the players quickly motivated the fans in the stands to join them. From there it took over the crowd like a wildfire. Indeed, wildfire is what it became. In the frenzy someone set fire to the stands. In no time the entire ballpark was ablaze. Players and fans alike had to evacuate the stadium. A few hours later all that remained of a once great ballpark were smoldering ashes and hot metal framework. Even worse, the fire spread to the surrounding business district. Eventually over one hundred other Boston buildings suffered severe damage. Some, like the ballpark, lay in a heap of ashes. Hundreds of people who worked in those buildings found themselves without jobs. That is what can happen when two people fight over something not worth remembering and a crowd gets out of control.

I like crowds. I am a speaker. Let me let you in on a professional secret: Public speakers rarely if ever brag about small crowds. We would rather address a large gathering than a small one any day. Preachers like big crowds. Any preacher who denies that is not being truthful. It is not unheard of for preachers to inflate the size of the crowd when they preach.

An old story tells about two preachers discussing their Sunday congregations. One said he usually had about two hundred fifty people come to hear him preach. The second, from a similarly sized church, said he never had less than three hundred, then, as conscience got the better of him, he quickly added, "Evangelastically speaking, of course." He coined a new word by combining the words evangelism and elastic as a ready made admission that some preachers fall for the temptation to stretch numbers when they count people in congregations. There is something exhilarating about a crowd, especially if you are a preacher.

As the old song says, *I Love A Parade!* A crowd on the march, that is, a procession, is almost always more stirring than a still one. The only exception to that might be when there is an offering involved, such as in church. It is hard to collect from everybody when people are on the move. Otherwise, however, a parade is better almost every time. I learned to march early. As a youngster, I graduated through the ranks from Life Boys, to Boys' Brigade, to the 6th Battalion of the Royal Ulster Rifles Territorial Army marching band. In each organization we marched through neighborhoods and city streets. In the Royal Ulster Rifles we wore hob-nailed boots with spit-and-polish toes and metal tapped heels. When we marched you could hear us coming. Let someone be a split-second out of step and everybody knew it, especially, it seemed, our Regimental Sergeant Major. He usually had some choice words for anyone who was not totally in-step. We were the South Down Militia, a proud regiment with a great history in the army of the Queen of England and he wanted us never to forget that. We were the Queen's own and she could call us into service at a moment's notice. We were ready, aye ready. The words of our regimental marching song swelled our chests with pride:

You can talk about your Grenadiers and gallant Forty-Twa,
But the South Down Militia is finest of them all!

In those days, few things excited me more than donning my neatly tailored bottle-green uniform, with its patent leather shoulder belt, plumed-peaked hat and those spit-and-polish marching boots. I loved those boots. I especially loved the clip-clip-clip sound that came from making sure the heel hit the ground in a certain way. We marched in smart formation through the streets of whatever city or town we were in at the time. Sometimes we accompanied members of the British Royal family on tours through Northern Ireland; once it was the Queen Mother, another time it was Prince Charles. People thronged the streets when British Royalty came in those days and whatever gathered a crowd was okay by me. Perhaps it is those memories that help make the Bible scenes of Palm Sunday exhilarating for me. If I let my imagination wander just a bit, I can see us there, decked out in our bottle greens complete with plume in hat, leading that parade into Jerusalem with the King of Kings and His entourage riding back somewhere near the middle.

The Mob Mentality

"The chief priests moved the people." What does it take to stir up a crowd? Not very much. Often just one passionate, articulate communicator can do it. Before you know it you have a rabble that thinks it has a cause.

Think, for example, about more recent sporting events than that one in Boston. Fans in Europe and the United States often whip themselves into a frenzy when their team wins a championship, or when referees rule in ways they do not like. Boston is not the only city whose sporting history bears the shameful, painful scars of an unruly mob.

Sports, however, do not have a monopoly on mobs run amok. Think, for instance, about what happened in Guyana when Jim Jones persuaded more than nine hundred people that drinking strychnine laced Kool-Aid was acceptable religious behavior. Similarly, a Japanese cult leader persuaded his devotees to release poison gas throughout the Tokyo underground transportation system, killing several passengers and injuring hundreds more. More recently, across the United

States, the mesmerizing eyes, calmly confident voice, and devious charm of Marshall Herff Applewhite gathered a following. Finally, in a rented home in an affluent Rancho Santa Fe neighborhood, Applewhite led the seemingly intelligent members of the Heaven's Gate cult down the road to Hell. They committed suicide with a perverted cocktail of vodka and Phenobarbital.

Others become excited over talk-radio. A popular personality takes on a cause. Before you know it, a multitude of listening disciples joins him or her. Soon, each one tries to outdo the others as the cause takes on a life of its own. Rush Limbaugh, the effervescent talk show host, found his fans often called in with similar compliments about his positions. To avoid repetitiveness, Rush suggested they simply say, "Ditto," when they agreed with his opinions. Soon people called trying to outdo one another with superlatives. "Double dittos" and "Mega dittos," none of which Rush declined, became the norm, and who among us would do differently if we were in his position? There is something about the human psyche that makes the accolades of the crowd intoxicating in their own way. It is easy for some of us to become entangled unwittingly in the mob mentality. We do it, I suspect, for a variety of reasons.

Sometimes it is our desire for inclusion. None of us enjoys being lonely, or feeling left out from the crowd, so we go along. Think, for example, of how quickly new fashion trends appeal to the masses. Recently USA Today, in a special report, covered the latest tattoo phenomenon. The most frequent reason people gave for being tattooed was their compulsive desire to look like their indelibly marked friends. They said they did not want to be the odd-one out among their tattooed peers. That mentality moves people to follow the leader in crowds that do both good and bad things.

Another Kind of Crowd Control

Crowd control usually means making certain a large group of people does not get out of hand, but it can mean something else too. Not long ago the Ku Klux Klan marched through our town. Barricades erected along City streets made Pittsburgh look more like Belfast or Beirut on a bad day than the City of Three Rivers. City employees installed a two-hundred-feet long chain-link neutral zone in front of City Hall to keep the Klan and their opponents from attacking each other. It was, in the words of the mayor, "crowd control."

Crowds can also wield amazing control over individual lives, not only in fashion trends but also in other behavior patterns. A newspaper reporter interviewed an old time circus headliner called, "Cannonball." In his heyday, Cannonball, blasted out of a circus cannon, flew through the air for several hundred feet as the crowd roared their approval. Even though he landed in a safety net that was set up to catch him each time the cannon spit him out, it was a very high risk exercise. "Why did you endanger your life like that?" the reporter asked. Immediately Cannonball replied, "Have you ever experienced hearing the applause of thousands of people every day and knowing it was all for you? That is why I did it." Whether Cannonball realized it or not, he was saying that he followed the crowd that followed him. He was under the spell of their approval. That, too, is crowd control, of a different type. In Cannonball's case, the crowd controlled him.

The Amorphous Mob

Cannonball took advantage of the circus crowds to fill his need for adrenaline and acceptance, and the thousands who watched him fly through the air were not disappointed. People gathering in large groups are neither a bad thing nor a good thing. It is their behavior when they come together that determines whether their impact is positive, negative, or neutral. Gathering for a baseball game is a good thing, but when the crowd becomes a fighting, arson practicing rabble that is something altogether different.

"Seeing the multitudes, he went up into a mountain" (Matthew 5:1). Jesus, too, took advantage of crowds throughout His earthly ministry, but for a different reason. That should not surprise us. After all, He was a preacher and no preacher wants to preach to himself.

In keeping with their Master's example, the disciples also liked addressing large crowds. Think, for example, of Pentecost: *"Peter...lifted up his voice...and the same day there were added unto them about three thousand souls" (Acts 2:14,41).* Three thousand new converts! Fantastic! No one has ever questioned if that number was reached by counting "evangelastically." You can be sure it was not.

Not long before Pentecost, *"The chief priests moved the people"* for a different reason. They were plotting the destruction of Jesus and they knew they could never do it alone, so they developed a strategy. In a few days, a few people with a cause they were persuaded was right, incited the Palm Sunday cheerleaders to become a murderous mob. The crowd that once had chanted, "Hosanna," would be turned to cry, "Crucify Him and give us Barabbas!" It was probably not a sudden transformation. It most likely began with a few determined disciples of the chief priests who used their influence and energy to shout down anyone who opposed them. The masses quickly fell into line in order that they would not feel out of place.

History is filled with the treacherous influence of a few inflexible zealots who carefully choreographed the behavior of the masses. Trotsky, Stalin, Hitler, Castro, Amin, are just some of the twentieth century perverted leaders whose names come to mind. Each, in his own way, knew how to gather a following and move a crowd for his own selfish ends. It is not hard for a few people to move a crowd, one way or another. Once on the march it is hard for followers to break ranks. In such a setting, a crowd can be a fierce and compelling thing. Self-restraint, stability, and decency can be compromised quickly in a crowd, if one is not careful. The fights and fires in Boston and the television news pictures of bodies lying on the ground in Jonestown, Guyana, are ample evidence of that.

The Mob Make-up

"They that went before, and they that followed, cried, saying, Hosanna" (Mark 11:9). Mark gives us a timeless spiritual word picture. It is worth noting that those farthest from Jesus shouted loudest. It is easy to drift away from Christ, lose His spirit and still call His name. Every generation in Christian history had certain personalities who were persuaded they had a monopoly on truth. Again and again, they ran ahead of God to accomplish their goals, often through forked tongues and fast drawn conclusions.

Mark's gospel reminds us that the people we walk with, and how they influence our behavior, is more important than all our words and causes. In the Palm Sunday parade, a quiet group marched near the Master. They did not shout or scream. Mark remembers that it was only, *"They that went before, and they that followed"* who were yelling. Our best hours with Jesus are not necessarily those when the crowd cheers us along. They are more likely to be the ones we spend quietly in His presence listening for the grace He would impart to our souls if only we would walk close and listen.

As Christians we are the *ecclesia.* That Greek word for church is a compound of two other words meaning to be called out from something. As disciples of Jesus, we are called out from the crowd to follow only One. That involves learning to think for ourselves and acting in ways that honor Christ, the Lord of Calvary. Popular opinion no longer holds sway over us. The only opinion that matters is the opinion of Him who called us and gave Himself for us.

With whom are you walking and how are you being influenced? The best evidence of that is seen in what we think and do as we walk. Walk close to the Master. Listen carefully for the pearls He would impart to your heart and heed His voice. Following Him closely, you will always be in the right crowd.

Our Spiritual Nikes

Thanks be to God, which giveth us the victory
through our Lord Jesus Christ.

−1 CORINTHIANS 15:57

*R*adio commentator, Paul Harvey, told a wonderful story about an Italian sailing team that went to Australia to participate in the America's Cup. Gucci, the famous Italian designer, outfitted the entire team in his latest sportswear fashions. They flew down-under as the best dressed team of them all. Upon their arrival they had some free time. They discussed what to do and decided they would like to see a kangaroo. They rented a Land Rover and proceeded into the bush. They not only saw a kangaroo, they bumped into one—literally. No one saw where it sprang from; but there it sat, upright and semi-stunned in the middle of a worn down, pot-holed, bush-country track. It looked like a photo-op made in heaven. They took lots of pictures. The driver thought it would be cute if he dressed the kangaroo in his Gucci jacket and took its picture for their designer. He put his jacket on the animal. They all laughed. The driver stepped back and aimed his camera. This would be the prize photo of the trip. Gucci would be delighted, he thought. At that moment, the stunned kangaroo revived and hopped away so fast that none of them could catch up with it. Paul Harvey concluded by saying that somewhere in the Australian outback today a very nicely attired kangaroo hops around the bush country with Land Rover keys in his pocket.

As Christians, we too are dressed in a high-class outfit that was provided by someone else. We also carry keys we did not earn. Ours is the robe of victory and in our pockets are the keys to God's kingdom. So says Paul, the apostle, *"Thanks be to God, which giveth us the victory through our Lord Jesus Christ."*

Christ's Resurrection Is Victory over Death

Through the lens of imagination, I see certain similarities between that yachtsman, the kangaroo, and Satan and us. How full of himself Satan must have been on Friday afternoon. He and his emissaries worked hard for a long time, laying their plans carefully. They moved the religious leaders to jealousy, and Judas to impatience. They melted the disciples' courage like snow on a hot tin roof. They turned the cheering Palm Sunday crowd to cry, "Crucify Him!" Jesus Christ, as dead as death can make someone, was taken from a rough Roman cross and laid in a tomb. Politicians were conscripted to put an official seal on His "final resting place." Armed guards were posted outside it to make sure there was no funny stuff by Christ's followers. Now Satan had Jesus in his jacket, the cloak of death.

That's right! The devil had the Lord of glory where he wanted Him.

Yet, when Easter morning came, the once dead Christ was resurrected. After rising again from death, He slipped away at a pace Satan can never match. *"I am he that liveth, and was dead; and, behold, I am alive for evermore, Amen; and have the keys of hell and of death" (Revelation 1:18).*

In Paul's power-filled words, *"Death is swallowed up in victory" (1 Corinthians 15:54).* Every angel in heaven laughs enthusiastically, *"Victory!"* Victory for the Son of God, and, because we belong to Him, victory for us.

Throughout this powerful resurrection chapter, 1 Corinthians 15, Paul responds to doubt-filled questions that made the rounds of Corinthian gossip groups. Those questions dared not challenge Christ's resurrection. There was too much evidence, and there were too many witnesses to call it into question. They questioned the ripple effect of that resurrection in our deaths. They said, "It is one thing to say Jesus rose again but what difference does that make for us when we die?"

Two cultural backgrounds fed the Corinthian understanding: Those of Jewish heritage, influenced by the sad-sack teaching of the Sadducees, said there is no life after death. (So, they were "Sad-you-see!") Jewish theology offers little hope for life beyond the grave. There is Sheol, sometimes inaccurately rendered, "Hell," in our English translation Bibles. Sheol is a gray netherworld where the dead are said to live a shadowy existence of no substance, no strength, no light, no hope. *"In the grave who shall give thee thanks?" (Psalm 6:5). "For the grave cannot praise thee, death can not celebrate thee: they that go down into the pit cannot hope for thy truth" (Isaiah 38:18).*

Generations of Israelites learned this theology of hopelessness from their religious teachers and philosophers. They believed it. In Corinth, as in your town, it was, and is, hard to replace old ideas with new thoughts no matter how good or true they may seem.

The Greeks, on the other hand, had an almost instinctive death fear that invaded the Corinthian mindset. Euripides wrote, "Mortals, burdened with countless ills, still love life. They long for each coming day, glad to bear the things they know, rather than face death the unknown."

That is pretty morbid, is it not? He says the suffering of this life is better than the unknown of what comes next. It reminds me of the woman who told an anguished friend in my wife Barbara's presence, "God is allowing all this to happen to you now to prepare you for something even worse that lies ahead of you." It was hardly the comfort she needed. Was it true? Well, only God knows that. Combine Euripides' conclusion with the Greek fascination with the human body which is perhaps best described as a love-hate relationship and there is not much comfort there either. They saw themselves as dead men walking. One Greek proverb likens the human body to a tomb.

Oh, but how far different death is for Christians! Jesus Christ, by His resurrection, leads us to life forever. He gives us hope. Paul declares with absolute certainty, *"For to me to live is Christ, and to die is gain" (Philippians 1:21).*

In his first letter to the Corinthians, the same Paul answers the question of the relationship between Christ's resurrection and ours by giving death a synonym neither Jew nor Greek thought of before. Paul uses the words for death and sleep interchangeably. He taunts death: *"O death, where is thy sting? O grave, where is thy victory?"* Death is an awful monster, but its sting has been removed.

Easter 1997 presented a special challenge for me. For one thing, it was our first Easter after my dad died and, although we did not know it at the time, it would be our last Easter with my mother. I chose my Easter text for 1997 in Ireland a few days after my dad's funeral. It was July 1996. As I planned my preaching schedule for the coming year, I became aware for the first time that I would be expected to preach on what would have been his seventy-seventh birthday, March 27, 1997, which was Maundy Thursday.

As I planned my preaching schedule, I suspected 1997 would be a tough Easter for me to bring good news to my people. Then I began to see Easter and death as the Bible portrays them from a new perspective. I had conducted hundreds of funerals over the years of my ministry, but now I was seeing Easter through the eyes of a painful personal grief. Long ago my dad and I had determined that the width of the Atlantic Ocean would not be allowed to hinder a wonderfully close relationship continuing between us. After Barbara and I emigrated to the United States Dad and I stayed in touch by every means available. Through my grief I could see that an angel of Christ slipped into that hospice room where my dad spent his final days and carried him across heaven's stoop like a new bride. My dad found death stingless. He saw the victory Jesus prepared for him: *"Death is swallowed up in victory... Thanks be to God, which giveth us the victory through our Lord Jesus Christ."* Because of the victory Jesus won, I shall see him again in glory. Christ's resurrection is victory over death.

But it is even more than that:

Christ's Resurrection Is Victory over Life!

Paul writes in the present tense: H *"giveth* (not, "will give") *us the victory through our Lord Jesus Christ."* Paul wants us to know Christ's victory is for this life also.

There were trials and temptations in Corinth over which the people needed help. It was not an easy time to be a disciple. It was a time like ours. It is never an easy time. Jesus says, *"In the world ye shall have tribulation: but be of good cheer;*

I have overcome the world" (John 16:33). From the catacombs of Rome to the secularism of our age, Christians have always been targets for every trouble hell can devise.

Yet, we know every challenge, every trial, and every temptation we face today was remembered on Calvary's cross and conquered in Christ's resurrection. There is power in Jesus to conquer every sin, every addiction, every lust, every hurt, every crisis, every broken heart this life can fling in our direction. To really believe the resurrection victory is to seize it here and now in the face of all these things. *"Be ye stedfast, unmoveable, always abounding in the work of the Lord, forasmuch as ye know that your labour is not in vain in the Lord" (1 Corinthians 15:58).*

Spiritual depression is public enemy number one in America today. The spirit of defeat I read on faces all across our nation, and in our city, breaks my heart. In politics, labor relations, education, inter-personal relationships, and the press, America has a worried look. Moreover, there is a latent hostility that lies close to the surface with too many of us. Some of us are ready to fight and argue at the drop of a hat. We raise people to great heights in government and business and then sadistically tear them apart. The same is true in the church. Renowned atheist Madelyn Murray-O'Hare even noticed it. "The Christian church," she said, "is the only army in the world that shoots its own wounded." That hostility, whether in the church or in society, is the child of personal depression. Among Christians, it denies the resurrection because it comes from an attitude born of defeat rather than victory. That is a tragedy in America the beautiful.

My love for my adopted country and her people makes me want to scream, "America, nation under God with liberty and justice for all, who is this God your coins tell me you trust? Do you really believe in the victory? If so, why are you so against one another? Why do so many of your people carry oppressed facial expressions? Why do you let your problems get on top of you? America, claim this victory for yourself and your people!"

If we really believe in Jesus Christ and His resurrection victory, why do so many of us live with lingering hostilities? Why can we not bring them to the cross and leave them there? Why are so many living defeated lives?

Put on Your Nikes and Run the Race!

The word Paul uses for *"victory"* is one we all know. In advertising it is represented by a logo that research indicates is among the most recognized by our young people. It is the Greek word, *nike.* It is the noun form of the same root as the Greek verb for *"overcome."* John uses the noun and verb forms in tandem: *"Whatsoever is born of God overcometh the world: and this is the victory that overcometh the world, even our faith" (1 John 5:4).*

John word choice means continually overcoming in the sense of running a marathon race. In short, the victory is guaranteed because we believe in it enough that we will hang tough until we claim it at the finishing post. We will overcome!

If I was to ask you today what problem in your life, your city, our nation, you would tackle if you knew victory was guaranteed, what would your answer be?

Here is the good news: Victory is assured. We have already overcome. We can do what needs to be done to turn any circumstance around. Christ has made His victory ours: *"But thanks be to God, which giveth us the victory through our Lord Jesus Christ. Therefore, my beloved brethren, be ye stedfast, unmoveable, always abounding in the work of the Lord, forasmuch as ye know that your labour is not in vain in the Lord."*

So, put on your spiritual *nikes* and run the race for the crown that Christ has set before us. And to God, who for Christ's sake redeemed us, be all the glory!

Presbyterian Potatoes Are the Same

He maketh his sun to rise on the evil and
on the good, and sendeth rain on the just
and on the unjust.

−MATTHEW 5:45

*E*ven the wheelchair that moved Bob Davis most of his waking hours for the last thirty-four plus years of his life could not conceal his football player profile. He was a hulk of a man by any standard. At age seventeen, in a high school game in

Bakersfield, California, Bob was tackled for the last time. When the coach ran onto the field he sensed immediately that something was very, very wrong. In an instant, Bob was paralyzed from the neck down by a spinal cord injury. The days that followed in the hospital intensive care unit provided treatments that saved Bob's life but could do nothing to restore power to his arms or legs. Below his neck Bob's hulk-like body was frozen and, for him, immovable. So much talent, so much to offer, but a moment of tragedy playing the sport he loved most took it all away. Some football players end up with multi-million dollar contracts. Bob, orphaned at age five, ended up with a wheelchair. Does God play fair?

"He maketh his sun to rise on the evil and on the good, and sendeth rain on the just and on the unjust."

Presbyterian Potatoes

If someone, somewhere, can tell without foreknowledge whether the potatoes we buy at the market were grown by a Presbyterian or a pagan I would like to meet that person. Is it fair that a Presbyterian farmer's potatoes are usually no better than those produced by a pagan farmer? Just a little bit more favored treatment with rain and sunshine could make the Presbyterian potatoes more desirable and command a higher price for the faithful farmer. Couldn't they even look better? Why does a good crop year benefit both pagan and Presbyterian farmer alike?

Simply because, *"Evil and good, righteous and unrighteous"* all receive the same treatment from God.

Why is the way of Christians not paved with blessing, and the trail of the unrighteous not filled with tears? It seems to me that nobody, certainly nobody in God's camp, would complain about that; and it could be a powerful evangelism tool. But God does not think so, or it would be that way.

Sometimes we use this way of thinking to wrongly accuse ourselves. Chuck Colson told about a nine year old New York boy who believed for a long time that he was responsible for a blackout. It seems that not long before the lights went out he kicked a power pole in a moment of anger. We smile at the idea, but many adults carry similar unjustifiable guilt throughout their lives.

Here's Mud in Your Eye!

"As Jesus passed by, he saw a man which was blind from his birth. And his disciples asked him, saying, Master, who did sin, this man, or his parents, that he was born blind? Jesus answered, Neither hath this man sinned, nor his parents: but that the works of God should be made manifest in him" (John 9:1-3).

The question the disciples asked Jesus that day was typical of the logic of the world they lived in, and that we live in at the present time. The common Jewish belief held that suffering and affliction was always the result of some great sin. Whose sin was it? They wanted, as we often do, a rule book of neatly packaged justice that answered all their "why" questions.

John's Gospel chapter 9 records six different reactions surrounding the blind man and his healing:

The disciples analyzed: *"Why is he blind?"*

The neighbors skepticized: *"Isn't this the one who begged?"*

The Pharisees criticized: *"This Jesus does not keep the Sabbath!"*

His parents, fearing excommunication, ostracized: *"He will speak for himself!"*

The blind man was revitalized: *"One thing I know, I was blind but now I see!"*

Jesus met his need: *"He took mud and put it in his eyes!"*

Never one to lose an opportunity, Jesus also seized the moment to teach a great truth. Was this man born blind

75

as punishment for sin? This is not a world of easy answers, He told them. Following that, He proceeded to heal the man with a miracle mud-pack from the Jesus Cosmetic Corporation, nineteen hundred years before Max Factor was born!

The Lord who later demonstrated on the cross just how upside-down our traditional ways of thinking can be, wants us to know that in this fallen world good behavior is not always rewarded and bad behavior is not always punished; at least, not yet. Sometimes Christians suffer while pagans prosper because the message of Christ is not about health and wealth as payment for faithful discipleship.

This Is Not a World of Judgment but of Probation

Something about the human nature of the best of us makes us too often quick to castigate and slow to approve. We are more ready to condemn than to commend. We savor evil stories, repeat gossip, and consume one another with our tongues. We quickly judge some people cruel and others charitable on the basis of very limited knowledge. Jesus saw that repeatedly in His disciples and used the blind man to teach us that life cannot be simply done up in neatly packaged philosophies.

Meanwhile, God, the real Judge and the only Judge who matters, says, "I will not pass judgment on you yet." He also uses equally distributed sun and rain to demonstrate His patience. In doing so, He also reminds us that as long as someone lives there is hope for that soul to be brought to the knowledge of the truth found only in Jesus.

Take the Lesson of Grace to Heart!

Judge slowly and forgive generously. *"Let every man be swift to hear, slow to speak, slow to wrath: For the wrath of man worketh not the righteousness of God" (James 1:19,20).*

An old fairy tale tells about a woman with two daughters; one compassionate, the other crabby. One day the mother sent the good daughter to a village well to fetch water. There she met a poor, elderly woman who asked for a drink. The girl spoke pleasantly and gave her a drink. The old woman, really a fairy in disguise, felt so blessed she gave the nice daughter a gift: "From now on your every word will be a jewel or flower falling from your lips."

Back home, the mother chastised her daughter for taking so long to fetch water. As the girl tried to explain the reason for her delay, a diamond, two pearls, and three rose petals fell from her lips. Her amazed mother immediately assigned the bitter sister to go after water from the same well. She reasoned that if a blessing can happen once, it can happen twice. True to form, the nasty sister grumbled all the way to the village well. The fairy, now disguised as a beautiful, wealthy woman, met her there and asked for a drink. The rude sister refused with abruptness. She, too, received a reward from the fairy: "Henceforth, each time you speak frogs and snakes will come out of your mouth."

We like stories like that because they portray instant justice, and we can go along with that. Commit a sin and get zapped! We call them fairy tales because that is not usually the way this world functions. None of us can afford instant justice. What we all need is mercy great and grace free.

The Happy Whistler

Bob Davis went to heaven not long ago. He was fifty-two years old. If Bob ever complained, I never heard about it. Injured at seventeen, he determined almost immediately that only his body was paralyzed. Over the next thirty-five years he proved it. His mind was always sharp and his heart was always set on doing good. Upon being sent from the hospital to a rehabilitation center, he quickly recognized that many other residents with similar injuries lived in a state of despair. To build their spirits, Bob started the Sunlighters' Club to inspire them. He was the first president. Thirty-five years later the Sunlighters are still lifting spirits there.

When he was well enough, he insisted on going back to his old high school where he completed his studies and graduated. He was accepted at nearby Bakersfield College where he studied for two years before being recruited to the University of California at Berkeley, from which he graduated with honors. At Bakersfield, Bob learned he could not attend football games because there were no handicapped facilities. When someone suggested rolling him onto the field, the official board overruled that idea for safety reasons. Not to be stopped, Bob started a fund raising drive. Sufficient money was raised to install facilities at the sports arena for people who were banned from games because of their handicaps. Each year at Bakersfield, Bob's inspiring leadership is remembered with a special program featuring his photograph on the front cover. At Berkeley he led the way in opening that school for handicapped students.

Those of us who knew and loved Bob called him "The Happy Whistler" because his joyful whistle told the story of a real-life hero whose spirit was never willing to be imprisoned in a wheelchair. It made no difference how ill he was; whether in the intensive care unit at Alta Bates Medical Center, with his friends at church, or at the home he shared with Sharon his loving wife, whom he met in the rehabilitation center where she worked, Bob was a source of encouragement and inspiration. He was always willing to accept his circumstances and grow with them as much as possible. He kept his mind active through the use of books and audio and video tapes. With words, smiles, or the twinkle in his eye, *"The work of God was displayed in his life."*

Through the path of humble acceptance and obedient discipleship he achieved a happier and more useful life within very restricted circumstances than many people ever manage to accomplish with excellent physical health. I know that as Bob walked (yes W-A-L-K-E-D!) through heaven's gates with his broad smile, and waved his arms for the first time in thirty-four years at friends, already there, who had never seen those arms lifted unaided before, he knew for certain now that the God He trusted is not unfair.

Bob realized quickly after his football career ended that day in 1962, that life only seems unfair when we forget to factor in God's grace and God's timeless justice. When we look at life without God, we see it with very short-range vision. God, on the other hand, sees it all from the perspective of eternity. *"And we know that all things work together for good to them that love God, to them who are the called according to his purpose" (Romans 8:28).*

Presbyterian potatoes are the same. It's what we make out of them that makes the difference!

The Big Blessing of a Little Theology

The secret things belong unto the LORD our God:
but those things which are revealed belong
unto us and to our children for ever, that we
may do all the words of this law.

-DEUTERONOMY 29:29

A dad and his lad were out walking one day when the lad asked how electricity could travel through wires stretched between telephone poles.

"I don't know," dad replied, "never understood electricity."

A few blocks further along the lad had another question: "Dad, what causes lightning and thunder?"

"I don't know," dad replied, "never understood weather."

Next it was airplanes: "Dad, how does a plane stay up in the sky?"

"Don't know. Never understood aeronautics."

Near home the lad said, "Dad, I hope you don't mind me asking questions."

"Not at all, son," Dad replied. "You gotta learn somehow!"

In Deuteronomy, Moses speaks about knowing and about not knowing: *"The secret things belong unto the LORD our God: but those things which are revealed belong unto us and to our children for ever, that we may do all the words of this law."*

A certain plague in modern Christendom stems from the passion of some people to define what God has left undefined; to attempt to tell what He has chosen not to tell. Such pursuit of spiritual minutiae is a form of godliness without power. Unrestrained, it often dampens the enthusiasm and impedes the witness of new believers who do not think they know enough to share the excitement of the new birth. Congregations have split, lifelong Christians relationships have been strained beyond the breaking point, and our united strength and witness for Christ has been hurt over theological incidentals.

Not long ago we boarded a plane on which some passengers were returning from a Bible prophecy conference. One fellow had purchased all the latest Bible software. Worse still, he had apparently stayed up all night the night before installing it on his notebook computer. The passenger next to him was obviously not a conferee. He demonstrated no interest in initial attempts to establish a conversation. Undaunted, the enthusiastic prophecy student turned on his computer and, for an hour and a half, attempted to dazzle his unfortunate seat-mate with knowledge neither of them really needed to know.

Prophecy Is Not a Plaything!

Every generation of Christians has had its prophecy buffs — people who have a penchant for predictions, but prophecy is not a plaything. Paul dealt with this among the Christians at Thessalonica, some of whom were so persuaded as to the soon coming of Christ that they left off their labors and looked up for the clouds to break. So Paul wrote his Second Thessalonian letter as a kind of corrective, to remind them that spiritual warfare rages all around us in the meantime and we prove ourselves worthy of Christ's coming by being about His business in the here and now.

When the Second World War was at its height, the Protestant theologian Dietrich Bonnhoeffer took his stand against the Third Reich and its leaders, especially Adolf Hitler. Bonnhoeffer was offered safe passage to a comfortable, and potentially prestigious seminary professorship in New York City. He declined on the grounds that Germany's Christians needed good pastors and scholars who were not afraid to stand against the evil tide that ruled in their country at that time. He made this decision knowing his position and his life were in peril every day that he stayed in Germany. Dietrich Bonnhoeffer was subsequently imprisoned, but Nazi prison bars could not restrain his passion for Christ and the gospel. He wrote and taught incessantly. His letters and papers were smuggled out from behind the barbed wire fences of the prison camp. They became a source of comfort and direction for the church for years to come.

Once a group of ministers who were convinced that Hitler was the Antichrist asked Dr. Bonnhoeffer, "Why do you expose yourself to danger? Jesus will return any day now, and all your work and suffering will be for nothing."

He replied, "You may be right, and if Jesus returns tomorrow, then tomorrow I will rest from my labor. But today I have work to do. I must continue with the struggle until it is finished."

Prophecy is not for playing. If God wanted us to know all things, he would have told us. What we are told is told to inspire us to work with the assurance that God, who has all the answers to all our questions, knows what we are about. He knows how much we know, and what we need to learn. Moreover, He promises to teach it to us. Jesus says, *"When he, the Spirit of truth, is come, he will guide you into all truth...He shall glorify me: for he shall receive of mine, and shall shew it unto you" (John 16:13-15)*. In Job's words, *"He knoweth the way that I take: when he hath tried me, I shall come forth as gold" (Job 23:10)*.

He also knows what He has determined is best kept from us, the *"secret things"* that are His alone.

Reverence for God and the word of God rules out conjecture about things that God has chosen not to make clear in His word. We must be content to know what Scripture tells us, and to respect what it does not tell us.

An witty Irish saint or scholar of long ago said, "Live each day as though it is your last and one day you will finally be right!" As Christians we have a duty to live each day as though it might be the day Christ will return, and to apply ourselves accordingly. And, one day we too shall be right! He will come and all knowledge will be made plain to all of us who trust Him.

"No man can at the same time give the impression that he is clever, and that Christ is mighty to save." Those words from the old English master preacher-statesman, John Henry Jowett, speak volumes to Christians in the information age. It is good to know all we can, only so long as we can use it to advance the work of Christ's Kingdom. It is also good to acknowledge that there are limits to the horizon of every aspect of human intelligence. God has chosen to keep some secrets and we show wisdom to respect that.

Why are some things secret?

Finite Minds Cannot Comprehend the Infinite

Our finite minds cannot fully understand the infinite aspects of God's nature. *"He hath set the world in their heart, so that no man can find out the work that God maketh from the beginning to the end" (Ecclesiastes 3:11).* Natural theology—what nature reveals about God—tells much, but is limited. Revealed theology—what the Bible tells about God—broadens our range of theological vision. It moves but does not erase the horizon.

God's book, the Bible, never claims to give us all the answers. It simply tells us enough to lift us above our intrinsic spiritual illiteracy and to direct us in His ways: *"That we may do all the words of this law.."*

In the Bible, God reveals His character: He is holy, just, merciful, compassionate, loving and bountiful. It makes plain that the only human being to perfectly replicate His moral attributes is Jesus, who died on a cross for our sins.

A wise theologian, known across the world for his brilliant mind, was asked by a press reporter, "What is the most profound thought about God to have ever entered your thinking processes?" Said he, "Jesus loves me, this I know, for the Bible tells me so."

His reply is astonishing because it is so simple and yet so profound. He could have bamboozled his inquirer with some deep theological concept, but he did not. Instead, he gave him a definition so simple little children can understand it.

At the end of life that small understanding of God and His Son, Jesus, is all the theology we need. The things we learn about God in Jesus, *"Belong unto us and to our children for ever.*" There are things we need to know revealed in Scripture. God gave them to us because we need them.

A godly professor and gifted scholar with a thorough knowledge of Scripture called on an outspoken student on the first day of class. "Mr. Watson," he asked, "do you have any problems with the Bible?"

"No, sir," he replied. "None!"

"Then you need to read it," replied the teacher. "Anyone who reads the Bible thoughtfully and honestly will be forced to raise questions about it."

Even Peter had struggles with reading the Scriptures. He declares with boldness that Paul's letters contain *"Some things hard to be understood, which they that are unlearned and unstable wrest, as they do also the other scriptures, unto their own destruction" (2 Peter 3:16).* Our difficulties with the Bible are not the result of Divine error so much as our limited human understanding.

But, the same Bible that tells so much about God's character hides His essence. He is more loving and wonderful than we can measure and so we define new theological terms in attempting to describe Him. We use words like omniscient, omnipotent, omnipresent and so forth. These terms, however, do not define God so much as they acknowledge the limits of our understanding. There are some things we cannot know and we should be content with that.

Be Satisfied with Secrets

The day will come soon enough when everything you have ever pondered with no final resolution will be revealed. That's right, one day you will be a know-it-all! The brilliant, scholarly Paul reminds us, *"Now I know in part; but then shall I know even as also I am known" (1 Corinthians 13:12).*

In the meantime, *"Be content with such things as ye have: for he hath said, I will never leave thee, nor forsake thee. So that we may boldly say, The Lord is my helper, and I will not fear what man shall do unto me" (Hebrews 13:5,6).*

Be blessed by your small theology as you determine to grow in the knowledge and love of God. Do not wait until you think you know everything for those who think they know everything, don't! Instead, with whatever learning you possess, go forth today and do the Lord's bidding!

A Bounteous Blindness

By faith Abraham, when he was called to go out into a place which he should after receive for an inheritance, obeyed; and he went out, not knowing whither he went.

–HEBREWS 11:8

"*When the Swallows Come Back to Capistrano!*" That grand old song's title and theme remind us how each year, for over one hundred and fifty years of recorded history, those swallows have come back to make their summer home in the eaves of the old San Juan Capistrano mission.

You can check your calendar by them. Some folks would even say you can set your watch. They always arrive on March

19, and depart on October 23. They never miss those dates, even in a leap year. Explain that! The best minds in science and ornithology scratch their heads in wonderment.

Is it some force of nature? Coincidence? Something to do with an indefinable thing called, "luck"? They cannot agree. Is it not more likely that God has created within those little golden-breasted creatures an instinct that tells them with supernatural exactitude when to head south and when to return to the north? All we know for sure is that each October 23, before daylight, the swallows wake earlier than usual, close up and leave. They seem to know exactly what they are doing, and where they are headed.

Abraham's Blind Adventure

What are you looking for? Where are you going? *"By faith Abraham, when called to go to a place he would later receive as his inheritance, obeyed and went, even though he did not know where he was going."*

Surely a bit of an explorer lies dormant in the soul of every truly-alive, thinking person. We are in love with places we have never seen and experiences we have not yet had. Old men dream dreams of what might have been. Young men have visions of what can be. Abraham was a hybrid of that idea. Even though old by any normal standard of measurement, he had a vision. Having had enough of the old place, he went forward where no one had ever gone before. He believed, rightly, that God was leading him. Many an immigrant to these shores can identify with him, for surely it is the vision of what might be that leads us to unfamiliar territories and new experiences.

Abraham is one of the Bible's great heroes, yet, he sometimes looked far removed from what most of us think of as a holy man. Middle East history until today testifies to some of the fruits of Abraham's impetuous ways. But above and beyond all that, *"Abraham believed God, and it was counted unto him for righteousness" (Romans 4:3).* Despite his occasional wayward ways, he truly wanted to do the right thing. Abraham was blind, but not sightless. He committed his life to a God bigger than himself, and aspired to please his God. He was not always successful, but he was always on his way. That is forever better than outward conformity to some code of inherited rigid purity because it holds a promise for improvement. In Abraham's case it indicated he was willing to grow and enlarge his mind, and thus his usefulness to God through his journeying. So, in the midst of his ho-hum Chaldean existence Abraham heard God's voice with a message, a mission and a call to his soul. *"He did not know where, but obeyed and went!"*

Life Is Best when Lived as a Blind Adventure

When we stop and really think about it, we realize that life is uncertain from the outset. It begins and ends that way. Despite what folk like Shirley MacLaine write, there is no serious evidence that any of us saw this planet before we were born. Nor have we seen where we are going after this. Having said that, the message of the Bible is clear that we can know for certain where that is.

Uncertainty is not a bane, but a blessing. When he set out on his blind adventure, Abraham had no idea whom, or what, he might encounter along the way, nor what would meet him. He could never have dreamed of all God had in mind for him. He had no notion of the way he would disgrace himself with a lie under pressure in Egypt, or his heart-wrenching family feud with Lot. His help-God-out affair with Hagar, the servant girl, and the day he would offer to sacrifice his son, Isaac, were not part of his pre-trip plans. If he had he might have quit before he started.

In the Parable of the Talents the Lord commends the people who are willing to take a risk to advance His work in the world. So it is in the life of each adventurer and risk taker. Ask the person who has built a successful business empire from scratch and you will hear the constant theme, "I had no idea it would ever be this big!" What we usually are not told is that they also had no idea of where their dream might lead them. If we stopped to tally the cost of every venture we would all stay in bed each morning, and maybe pull the sheets up over our heads. Life, however, is not meant to be lived inside the safe fences of what we already know and possess. Great discoveries in science and medicine are never made by reciting what we already know. Only by pushing out the boundaries of present knowledge do we make great strides into new realms that benefit all humanity.

Is there a risk in that? Of course! Is it possible to fail doing that? Absolutely! Does the possibility of tough times lie as yet undiscovered every time someone takes a risk for something good? Almost certainly! History is replete with stories of great people going through tough times to get to where they believed they needed to be. Abraham was one of them.

Yet, with all that, truly great achievers know that God uses the tough experiences to build character and direct our paths properly to the places He has planned for us. So it was with Abraham, and so it is with us. Thus, Paul the apostle tells the Romans, *"We glory in tribulations also: knowing that tribulation worketh patience; and patience, experience" (Romans 5:3,4).*

To commit oneself to serving Jesus Christ is to embark on a character building course. It is to take up a cross, just as He took up our cross. It is also to discover that crosses come in different shapes and sizes.

Life! The Ultimate Adventure!

As Christians, we know what we are looking for, but we are not sure where our search will take us. Walking with God is no guarantee of an easy road.

At the entrance to one of the parking lots at Pittsburgh International Airport, an automatic gate rises up and opens the way ahead. It happens every time a car passes a certain spot and activates a hidden sensor. Recently a fellow in the car ahead of me spotted the barrier and slowed to a dead stop a few feet before that sensor. Afraid of damaging his car, I suppose, he first studied the situation and, unable to see clearly what would happen if he moved ahead, he decided to park there. Never mind that there were other cars behind him, including mine! He decided that since he was unsure, he would go no further. Needless to say, the gate would never open as long as his car did not go forward. Only in moving ahead would the way open before him.

That is what faith is like. Sometimes you have to move ahead just a little bit before one of life's great plans opens up before you. Often our problem is that we want to see a blueprint finely drawn to completion when God's plan is a scroll He plans to unfurl one day at a time.

Missionary Virginia Law Shell tells the story of how, years ago, older men were employed as night sentries for jungle missionary homes. They swept yards, heated bath water, guarded houses, and carried messages between houses in the compounds in the darkness. It was not unusual, she remembers, to hear someone cough at the front door late at night. Experience taught that the cough signaled that one of the men was there, most likely with a message.

One night she recognized the familiar cough of Papa Jean, the sentry from the single women's dormitory. From the dim lamp he carried, she could see Papa Jean was holding a note in his hand. It was a dark, moon-less, star-less night and the lamp gave only a smattering of light.

"Your lamp doesn't give much light, does it Papa Jean," she smiled at him. "No, madam, it doesn't," he replied, "but, it shines as far as I can step."

Think on those words. God's lamp does not often shine as far as we might like it to, but it always shines as far as we can step. Abraham went out one step at a time and the lamp of the Lord shined farther for him, one step at a time.

Is some barrier blocking your path? Pretend it is not there, and move ahead a bit. God may lift it out of your way. *"Abraham...went out, not knowing whither he went."* But the Lord knew, and that was all Abraham needed. It is all any of us need.

11

When Success Gives Birth To Failure

*In that night did God appear unto Solomon, and
said unto him, Ask what I shall give thee.
And Solomon said unto God...Give me now wisdom
and knowledge, that I may go out and come in
before this people: for who can judge this thy
people, that is so great?*

−2 CHRONICLES 1:7,8,10

*W*hen a young woman of Ireland becomes engaged to be married it is customary for her to allow her not-yet-affianced female friends to try on her ring, not for size but for a delightful friendship ritual. Upon putting the ring on her third left-hand finger, each friend turns the ring three times on her finger and as she turns it she makes a secret wish. She can, at that moment, ask for anything except a husband for herself or great riches.

Once I asked a newly betrothed young woman this question: "Since you could wish for neither man nor money, what did you wish for each time you practiced that ring ritual?" Her reply demonstrated a fanciful imagination. Said she, "I simply asked for happiness. That way I'll get both man and money!"

Now, here is a question for you: If God asked you what you wanted, and assured you that whatever you asked for would be granted, what would you ask for?

God invited Solomon, *"Ask for whatever you want me to give you."* Solomon replied, *"Give me wisdom and knowledge, that I may lead this people."*

Solomon's Choice

God promised the twenty year old Solomon that any wish he wanted would be fulfilled. It was almost a dream too good to be true. Of all the things he might have asked for, Solomon asked for wisdom and knowledge to govern and guide the people over whom he would be king. On the surface, it sounds like a good thing to ask for. Solomon was young and had just taken on amazing power and responsibility.

If Solomon asked well, we must also say that God gave well. Solomon quickly developed a reputation for astute leadership. It was well deserved. Unfortunately, however, Solomon, sometimes called the wisest man who ever lived, also did some incredibly stupid things.

Solomon's Comeuppance

Solomon's folly lies subtly in his request; not so much in what he asked for, wisdom, which was a good thing, but in his motivation. *"Give me wisdom and knowledge,"* he prayed, *"that I may lead this people."*

Solomon's problem was that he sought to direct the lives of others before he learned to control his own life. In short, he forgot he needed to be a man before he could be a king. He asked for an ability to rule the lives of others without regard to who would control his own life.

Now, here is another question for you: Think about your answer to the first question. Why would you ask for that? The issue now is not what we would ask for, but why we would ask for it. Just as important as making a choice, is knowing why we make it. When we understand the reason for the choices we make in life, we begin to realize the forces that drive us.

The Inside War

In each of our lives, there is an inner kingdom and an outer kingdom. There are forces within us more powerful than any force outside us. Jesus said it is not the forces without that corrupt but those that are within. Paul reminds the Ephesians, *"Put off concerning the former conversation the old man, which is corrupt according to the deceitful lusts; and be renewed in the spirit of your mind" (Ephesians 4:22,23).*

History is filled with the stories of otherwise great leaders who forgot that. Alexander, Charlemagne, Napoleon and a host of history's leaders from the worlds of politics, business and even the church, were brought low by their corrupt inner kingdom. This kingdom within brings down dictators, presidents and monarchs in every generation. In our century, names such as Marx, Mussolini, Hitler, Khrushchev, Amin, Ceausescu and others come to mind. In every case they were possessed by a power more powerful than any army they ever commanded. It takes place every day, and at every level of leadership, whether politics or business. It even happens in the church. Church history is filled with accounts of corrupt leaders who by various illicit means and devices attempted to commandeer God's work in the world. Although none has ever succeeded some have made their mark, or, more correctly, their scar on the greatest work in the world. So, Scripture encourages us to remember leaders with urgency: *"I exhort therefore, that, first of all, supplications, prayers, intercessions, and giving of thanks, be made for all men; for kings, and for all that are in authority" (1 Timothy 2:1,2).*

But it is not only famous leaders who need to remember their own shortcomings. We must do it too, whether famous or obscure in the eyes of the world. We all wrestle against some weakness we would rather was not a part of us.

Solomon failed to recognize his fatal flaw. His libido, if not kept in check, would quickly run amok and lead to his downfall. It was the same problem that once led to an embarrassing moment in the life of his father, David.

David, seeing her sunbathing, was sensually aroused by Bathsheba's incredible beauty. The rest of the story, as they say, is history. David seduced her. Bathsheba, not at all an unwilling accomplice, soon found out she was expecting David's child. She subsequently stood by as David schemed the death of her husband, Uriah. That episode in the mighty David's history tells of the powerful domino effect of sin. It began with covetousness, a thought sin; wove its way through lying and deceit, sins of the lips; and ended up in adultery, betrayal, and murder, sins of the life. David lost his most valuable possession, his peace with God, which he later calls the joy of salvation.

Now, Solomon, son of the illicit relationship between David and Bathsheba, is being brought low by the same family demon that ensnared his father and mother. Like his father, on the surface Solomon looked successful, as a leader, a strategist, and as a lover. Unlike his father, Solomon seems never to have learned his lesson. No record shows he ever changed his ways. He thought to buy control of people by marrying into each royal family and took a new princess from each surrounding nation to be his bride and as a means of building his political influence. Soon he had 700 wives and 300 mistresses. Despite his successful looks he was digging himself into a deeper hole of failure every time he perpetuated his behavior pattern.

Solomon's wives and concubines controlled him. Each new bride or concubine entering his private quarters brought her own agenda. None of them cared for Solomon's good. Before it was over, one thousand and one wealthy, powerful people lived in high style in Solomon's royal palace. Amazingly, none of them was happy about their situation. In time, Solomon lost control of his own palace and the loyalty of his own kinsfolk citizens who despised the high taxes he imposed on them to sustain his lavish lifestyle. The moral of his story is that it is possible to "have it all" —money, sex, power—and still not be happy.

Solomon's Folly

Some people still wonder how anyone can appear to have everything and still not be happy? How can someone as smart as Solomon end up looking stupid? In his case it was that he overlooked his own weaknesses. Instead of majoring on restraining himself, Solomon prioritized regulating others. In trying to bring them under his power with the wise leadership he prayed for, he set his own desires first. His priorities were out of order. For you see, *"The kingdoms of this world"* (including Solomon's and yours!) really are *"the kingdoms of our Lord, and of his Christ; and he shall reign for ever and ever" (Revelation 11:15).* "How much of your wealth is yours and how much is God's?" a wag asked a wealthy wise man. "It is all His," he replied. Don't ever forget that and you will be counted wise in the face of this world's foolishness.

Smarter Than Solomon!

Christ Jesus, the Man who was, and is, smarter than Solomon, says, *"He that findeth his life shall lose it: and he that loseth his life for my sake shall find it"* (Matthew 10:39), and proved His integrity by pursuing that ideal even when it meant hauling a heavy cross along the Via Delorosa to the top of the hill called Calvary. The Lord of the cross says to our what's-in-it-for-me world, "If it is happiness you want, give yourself away." All the money, sex, and power in Solomon's world cannot secure it.

Today God says to us, *"Ask for whatever you want me to give you."*

Before you answer remember this, you are a person. You need Someone stronger than yourself to help you control your life. That Someone is Christ. Why not say, "God, give me grace to know your Son, the Lord of the cross, and to be like Him. Let me find, in Him, that true wisdom which leads to eternal life."

12

Not Hard to Make Happy

Without faith it is impossible to please him: for he that cometh to God must believe that he is, and that he is a rewarder of them that diligently seek him.

-HEBREWS 11:6

*H*is name, Christopher, means, "Bearer of Christ," yet he was anything but that throughout his adolescence and into early adulthood. As a young man, Chris came to believe his perfectionist father could not be pleased. Everything he attempted to do, no matter how hard he tried, his dad found cause to criticize. As a result, Chris grew up believing nothing he would do would ever be acceptable. As a middle school student, he received Christ but lived in a state of perpetual misery and hopelessness. He was convinced that if he could never satisfy his earthly father, he surely could never hope to appease his Heavenly Father. But, unlike some earthly fathers I've heard about, God is not impossible to please.

The Hebrews' writer says, *"Without faith it is impossible to please him: for he that cometh to God must believe that he is, and that he is a rewarder of them that diligently seek him" (Hebrews 11:6).* He does not say it is impossible to please God but that God cannot be pleased unless we have genuine faith.

What Faith Is

An atheist asked a believer, "Have you ever seen God? Or touched, or smelled Him?" When the believer acknowledged he had not, the atheist exclaimed in mock disbelief, "Then how can you be sure your God exists?" After a pause the Christian responded with a question of his own: "Have you ever seen your brains? Or touched, or smelled them?" When he had his accuser's attention the Christian asked, "Then how can you say your brains exist?"

Practical Atheism

True atheism in the sense of an intellectual position honestly reached after careful and adequate examination of all the relevant evidence is rare, if it exists at all. Few serious thinkers capable of adequately examining the evidence would commit themselves after such examination to declare with any degree of certainty, "There is no God." And the more science and the other disciplines of learning and research uncover, the harder it is to advocate that position and look intelligent.

Practical atheism, on the other hand, is far more prevalent among us. Practical atheism is not a mindset, but a way of life. It is atheism that is practiced despite what one says one believes. Where philosophical atheism says God does not exist, practical atheism gives God lip service whilst denying His existence in its lifestyle. While there are few, if any, true philosophical atheists, there are many authentic practical atheists. These are those people whose profession of faith in Christ's cross and resurrection, often hard-nosed, loudly verbalized and strongly advocated in front of friends, is denied by their half-hearted lifestyles. They exist without ever taking the risks true faith demands. Theirs' is that straw faith with no deeds which James calls useless *(James 2:20).*

"The fool hath said in his heart, There is no God" (Psalm 14:1). It is not those whose lips deny God who concern David, the psalmist, but those whose hearts and actions question God's existence by their lack of trust and negative spirits.

A noisy nightclub opened near a pleasant residential community on the outskirts of a great city. Some local church members promptly called an all-night prayer vigil. In prayer after prayer, they expressed their opposition to the intruding business. Someone even prayed, "Dear God, send a fire this very night to destroy that evil establishment." The plea sounded so earnest that a number of the hearers sped it on to heaven with their hearty Amen. Later they commended the one making the prayer as a truly faith-filled believer, a person of genuine faith. Amazingly, that very night an unexpected lightning bolt struck the intruding place of business, setting it on fire. It burned to the ground with a glory the prayer warriors secretly cherished in days to come. Upon hearing of that prayer meeting, the club owner filed a lawsuit against the Christians. In court he told a judge their prayer meeting was the beginning of his undoing. The Christians scoffed at his claim. "Who ever heard of such a thing," they exclaimed in horror. "Everyone knows that prayers like that are not answered." The judge, finding for the business owner, said in giving his verdict, "It seems to me that he is the real Christian for he believes in prayer more than all the Christians in this community!" They said they had faith, but in practice they were atheists, practical atheists.

Some Christians spend good hours every week in Bible studies and church but their lives and actions demonstrate the absent religion of the one David calls a fool. Vic, an outspoken elder in his church, does not trust God enough to tithe. His holding out demonstrates his true belief. Betsy talked a good game when other members of her Sunday School class were within earshot. On the other hand Betsy worries about almost everything. Vic and Betsy are practical atheists.

The faith heroes of the Bible are not like that. They are united in two ways. First, each of them is a flawed character. Their lives are often far from perfect. Some experienced a deep level of moral failure. The second way that they are united grows out of their response to realizing their human frailties: When put to the test they acted as though God might bring good through them, and He did. When confronted with their sins, they readily acknowledged them and repented. Such is the faith that pleases Him.

Faith That Makes God Happy!

Faith that pleases God is more than words. It is linking lips with life. It is acting on what we believe although we have not seen it. It is forsaking the obvious and the owned for that which, though not yet seen, is far more lasting.

Think, for example, about those Bethlehem shepherds keeping watch over their flocks by night. When their darkness was broken by the light of singing angels they made a decision that demonstrated true faith. Without regard for job security, they acted as though the message was true. As a result, they saw the Christ-child face to face. What a reward for faith in action!

There are people in every church congregation who have heard moving sermons about Jesus and His cross and are always looking for more of the same, but their faith has no sense of adventure. Unwilling to risk, they never demonstrate a willingness to forsake all that they have to follow Jesus.

Nickels and Noses

We apply that same rule of success to our churches. I call it the nickels and noses syndrome. It measures ministry success purely in terms of attendance numbers and budgets. Its secular counterpart is best defined by the bumper sticker that screams, "Whoever dies with the most toys wins!" But that is a far cry from what God is looking for from His church, or from us as persons. Such a measure of success never considers risking new ground. Abraham would never fit in a church like that for he, *"went out, not knowing whither he went" (Hebrews 11:8).* In going out blind, so to speak, he became God's hero.

In California's Anaheim a piece of farmland looked so ordinary no one imagined it could become an attraction for drawing families from all over the world together. No one, that is, except one man, a cartoonist-dreamer by the name of Walter Elias Disney. One day the dreamer shared his dream with others in such a way they could not resist it. Walt's Disneyland was such a success from the first day it opened that it is rather amazing some entrepreneur back east did not try to adapt Disney's dream to somewhere, say, like Central Florida, where the weather is good and the living is easy. Yet, no one did, until Walt Disney dreamed a bigger dream that put a small virtually unknown Florida hamlet called Orlando on the map forever. Walt Disney knew his new dream was so magnificent that it might not be completed until after his death. "Buy extra acreage so my successors will have room enough to grow," Walt counseled. The people around him questioned the wisdom of that statement; but they remembered who was the boss. Walt got his extra land. When Disney World opened in Florida in 1971, thousands of families celebrated.

Someone lamented, "It's kind of sad that old Walt didn't live to see this." But Walt did see it. He saw it through the eyes of faith. He saw it long before they did, before the ground was cleared to make way for the first building.

Such is the faith that pleases God. True faith is to support hospitals where we never expect to be sick. It is to build schools where we do not expect to be educated. It is to start churches where we may never worship. It is to feed and clothe and visit hungry and naked and undesirable people we may never meet.

Perhaps such faith is best summed up in these words, "Go as far as you can see, and after you get there you will always see farther." Faith that pleases God, *"Is...certain of what we do not see."* God is not pleased until we act as though we believe in what we have not yet seen, or touched, or smelled. It is not what we can count or calibrate that God measures, but what will become countable and measurable if we pursue the dreams He gives us. When we set sail for uncharted waters that advance the cause of Christ, God counts that as a mark of success and growth for us.

"Faith cometh by hearing, and hearing by the word of God" (Romans 10:17). His promise is that He rewards those who act upon what they hear through spiritual ears when the Spirit of Jesus whispers a new challenge. So go forth acting as though Christ's message is true and in time you will find your reward and God will be pleased.

A Sure Foundation

According to the grace of God which is given unto me, as a wise masterbuilder, I have laid the foundation, and another buildeth thereon. But let every man take heed how he buildeth thereupon.

–1 CORINTHIANS 3:10

"*T*he only certainty is uncertainty!" The television news commentator seemed to relish every word as he laid out his predictions for the future of Hong Kong. The citizens went to bed one night as people of the British Empire and awoke the next morning as citizens of the Chinese Republic. Critics said they had gone to bed free men and women and awakened under Communism's oppressive rule. It reminded me of that fateful Saturday night the Berlin Wall crumbled before the eyes of a world-wide television audience, except that something was strangely reversed about what was happening out in the Pacific.

That television commentator said that in this computer age nothing is certain any more. I suspect his prediction is on target. Life is changing at such a rapid—and some might say, "rabid" —pace that it is well nigh impossible for anyone to keep up with it all. If you keep a daily journal and record the changes that take place day by day you know what this means, at least in your corner of the world.

When we lived in San Mateo, in California's San Francisco Bay Area, we drove across the San Andreas Fault regularly. It was an experience to which one did not become accustomed quickly. The cemetery where many families from our church had their burial plots lay on the other side of the Fault from our church. I never quite conquered the eerie feeling of driving across that uncertain piece of ground in a slow funeral procession. Sometimes I would think, "Wow, what if today is the day this thing is going to vibrate, split and fall off into the Pacific as some seismologists predict it will one day?" I had visions of a whole funeral going underground or floating off into the ocean on a piece of California!

But, did you know that no matter where you live, the land beneath your feet is on the move? According to Smithsonian Magazine, scientists are studying crustal plates that are emerging at ridges deep beneath the oceans. It is believed that when these plates abut and lock together, the sudden release of accumulated stress causes earthquakes. That television commentator is right: "The only certainty is uncertainty."

One day, Jesus said, *"There shall be...earthquakes, in divers places" (Matthew 24:7)*. Jesus prepares us to expect the unexpected as a sign that this age is coming to an end. The recent spate of earthquakes in places we do not normally associate with such occurrences, such as Scotland, should cause us all to stop and take notice.

For some folk these events do not bring much comfort. For others they are merely signs of the times. However, there are some things that will not change.

Some Things Never Change

In the future, as in the past, there will be no free lunches. Don't expect something for nothing. Somebody always pays. This will never change.

Regardless of the splendid improvements in surgical procedures, exercise programs, and the cosmetics industry, you are not going to get any younger. You may look younger for a while, but the fact is, there are parts of you that are wearing out because the Manufacturer does not intend them to last forever. The psalmist David puts that idea a bit more judiciously in these words, *"My times are in thy hand" (Psalm 31:15).* In another Psalm Moses prays, *"So teach us to number our days, that we may apply our hearts unto wisdom" (Psalm 90:12).* In short, time is limited for each of us and we do well to make the most of it.

Is there something you are planning to do? Some goal you want to accomplish, but have put off doing? Better get to it! Set a plan in motion now before it is too late.

Here is another thing that will never change: God in heaven will always be in control of the universe. Nothing will happen in the course of this world or the next over which He does not have ultimate control. Moreover, no matter what happens, He will always be directing world affairs with the best interests of those who are His in mind. He promises that *"all things work together for good to them that love God, to them who are the called according to his purpose" (Romans 8:28).* You can count on that, no matter how the world appears to turn.

The Ten Commandments may be barred from the walls of public buildings in America, but they will never be ruled out of life's deepest core. We may not know what laws the United States Congress will pass, or which laws the United States Supreme Court might overturn, but God's Ten Laws will never change. Order your life around them and you will never have to deal with uncertainty.

This, too, is certain: Love will forever be the greatest force in the world. I do not mean the fickle, Hollywood kind of love; but the love of God, manifest in Jesus Christ, His Son, will accomplish more to positively transform lives than all the forces this world can muster.

Our Sure Foundation!

Above all else, Jesus will always be the best foundation on which to build your life.

My friend, Steve Brown, moved into his new home not long before Hurricane Andrew blew through Miami, Florida. The morning after the hurricane, every house in Steve's neighborhood, except one, lay in a heap of rubble. That one house was not Steve Brown's. It belonged to someone else. A television news reporter asked the owner of the only surviving house if he had any idea why his house withstood the storm when all the others lay in heaps of rubble around him. The man said simply and modestly, "Yes. I built this house myself and followed the Florida building code. The code called for two by six inch roof trusses. I knew some builders were convinced the code was too strict. They skimped by with two by fours, convinced they would be sufficient. Building inspectors were paid off for turning a blind eye to this discrepancy. I could have saved money doing that too, but I chose to take no chances."

Now there is a word for the wise: Take no chances. Build your life on the foundation God gives and the storms will never destroy you: *"For other foundation can no man lay than that is laid, which is Jesus Christ" (1 Corinthians 3:11).*

Take God at His Word

What shall we then say to these things?
If God be for us, who can be against us?

-ROMANS 8:31

*T*he beautiful Gothic cathedral-like building of First Presbyterian Church of Pittsburgh sits on land in the Golden Triangle. That land was left by William Penn's heirs for the advancement of the Christian faith. A copy of the deed hangs in a frame on the wall of one of our church offices. It tells the world how we received that ground. Someone told me how William Penn obtained that land. It makes a fascinating story and brings to mind a great Bible text.

The devout William Penn once described his life philosophy in these words: "Men must be governed by God or they

111

will be ruled by tyrants." It is said that Penn worked hard to demonstrate the integrity of that philosophy. As a result, unlike others in his time, he was able to develop a trusting relationship with the American Indians who formerly owned the land. As a result a strong bond developed between William Penn and a certain Indian chief. One day that Indian chief told the founder of Pennsylvania that he would give him as much land as he could walk off in a day.

William Penn responded without hesitation. Early next morning he started walking as fast as he could. He trudged over the hills and through the valleys of Western Pennsylvania until late in the evening. All day long he walked without stopping.

When the Indian chief heard about William Penn's walk, he was both impressed and flattered. First, he was impressed with how far William Penn had traversed that day. More than that, however, the Indian chief was flattered that a white man simply believed the word of an Indian. This happened at a time when the relationship between the early white settlers and the Indians was not one marked by trust. With every footstep he took that day, William Penn demonstrated a profound willingness to take the chief at his word.

Think about it: William Penn would have never owned the land and our church would not sit there had he not believed a promise. Now, what about God's promises? Paul climaxes the Golden Chapter by asking, *"What shall we then say to these things? If God be for us, who can be against us?"* In this one verse, Paul identifies three realities we must deal with:

An Identified People

"What shall we then say to these things? If God be for us, who can be against us?" Who are the *"We"* and the *"Us"* in Paul's proposition?

Romans chapter eight makes plain that these words are not for everyone. Paul has already described the subjects as people, *"No condemnation...Free from the law of sin and death...Who walk not after the flesh, but after the Spirit...To be spiritually minded is life and peace...Heirs of God, and joint-heirs with Christ" (see verses 1,2,4,6,14-17).*

The first natural question that arises is, "Are you one of us?" Do Paul's words throughout Romans 8 describe you? Do you belong to Jesus? William Penn took the Indian chief at his word. Have you taken the God who makes Himself known to us in Christ at His word? Do you stand on His promises? Or, merely sit in His premises? In short, are you a church attendee, or a bona-fide disciple? Only those who have believed and acted on God's promises qualify for inclusion among Paul's, *"We"* and *"Us."*

This leads us to the another point encompassed by Paul's statement:

An Illustrated Position

God, writes Paul, is *"for us."* The Bible gives wonderfully descriptive word pictures of how God positions Himself in relation to us. Consider just a few of them:

He is, for example, God *before* us. Moses remembers, *"The LORD went before them by day in a pillar of a cloud, to lead them the way; and by night in a pillar of fire, to give them light; to go by day and night" (Exodus 13:21).*

The picture is of Israel's children traveling out of their Egyptian bondage under divine guidance. Moses wants us to note that our God goes before us, leading the way. We can go nowhere that God has not preceded us.

For Isaiah, the prophet, He is God *with* us: *"The Lord himself shall give you a sign; Behold, a virgin shall conceive, and bear a son, and shall call his name Immanuel" (Isaiah 7:14).* The Hebrew word *Immanuel* means literally, *"God with us."*

John's Gospel highlights this relationship at the beginning of his testimony about Jesus. *"In the beginning was the Word, and the Word was with God, and the Word was God...The Word was made flesh, and dwelt among us" (John 1:1,14).* Similarly, David the psalmist underscores God's presence: *"Thou hast beset me behind and before, and laid thine hand upon me...If I ascend up into heaven, thou art there: if I make my bed in hell, behold, thou art there" (Psalm 139:5,8).* No matter where we go, God in Christ accompanies us. This is surely a source of great comfort to every follower of Jesus.

Nahum, the prophet, uses a wonderful language idiom that emphasizes God's place *around* us: *"The LORD is good, A stronghold in the day of trouble; And He knows those who trust in Him" (Nahum 1:7 - NKJV).*

On the Northern Irish coast not far from Belfast a towering castle catches the eye of everyone who passes it both by land and by sea. It is Carrickfergus Castle, the castle where William III, the Dutch Prince of Orange, arrived to lead the Irish people to victory against the evil King James II. The tall stone walls of Carrickfergus Castle are over two feet thick. For more than eight hundred years those walls have stood steadfast, a stronghold against every assault that warring nations could bring them. They still stand firm today, as strong as ever.

Do you realize a protecting force even more powerful than all those great stones protects you? Do you understand that no force on earth can harm you because God surrounds you by day and by night like a thick walled fortress? You are impenetrable!

God is not only before us, with us, and all around us. He is *in* us. Paul is so caught up by God's residence within us that he makes it a theme of each of his letters. Christ is, he notes, *"in"* us: *"Christ in you, the hope of glory" (Colossians 1:27).*

As wonderful as that is, it is not the end of it. Paul emphasizes that we are also in Christ. He writes of the amazing

114

difference this makes to our lives: *"If any man be in Christ, he is a new creature: old things are passed away; behold, all things are become new" (2 Corinthians 5:17).*

Each of these positions anthropomorphically demonstrates God's physical relationship to us. When Paul writes near the end of Romans Chapter 8, that God is *"for us,"* he moves into an even higher understanding of the relationship God assumes in Jesus. He goes from the physical realm to the spiritual one.

To emphasize the depth of God's spiritual commitment to us, Paul reaches for a strong Graeco-Roman military term. *Huper* is a Greek word that describes the level of commitment required of soldiers for their comrades. They are pledged to provide reinforcement for one another and, if need be, to give their lives and their sacred honor in defense of each other. God stands ready to defend us with His life.

That is, of course, exactly what God the Son did on the cross at Calvary. He gave His life for ours. With His support behind us we become an unbeatable force!

Think about it: You will never encounter a disappointment so dark, a hurt so horrible, a hurdle so high, that God's love in Jesus cannot, and will not, defend you in it and ultimately redeem it for your good. Whatever temptations or battles assail you, stand firm in the Lord and you will reap the victory. Say to every force of evil around you today and always, "Take your best shot. God will turn your evil into good for me!" *"If God be for us, who can be against us?"*

This brings us to the final point for emphasis:

An Intriguing Proposition

Think again about Paul's exciting opening interrogative: *"What shall we then say to these things?"* Such a question demands our response. Before you answer it, remember where Pittsburgh's historic First Presbyterian Church sits and how William Penn obtained that land.

The Things Christ Has in Mind

He himself knew what he would do.

−JOHN 6:6

*A*part from the resurrection of Jesus, only the miracle of the loaves and fishes excites all the gospel writers so that none of them feels Christ's story is fully told without it. An exciting missionary adventure of teaching and miracles was dashed by news of John the Baptizer's assassination. That heartbreaking news came at an especially taxing time. In an effort to achieve some rest and relaxation, Christ and His disciples retired across the lake called Galilee. That was the backdrop for an incredibly timeless human story that many of us first heard as children. Of all the gospel writers, only John writes that Jesus, *"knew what he would do" (John 6:6).*

The Things We Have in Mind

The disciples, even though they had witnessed many miracles in the preceding days, were frustrated when Jesus suggested feeding the multitude. It was a long way from any place to buy food and feeding five thousand people would be a costly exercise, they reasoned. They had no idea what the sovereign Christ *"had in mind to do."* Life is full of far-fetched demands for which our resources seem inadequate. The disciples would have sent the people away hungry. But Jesus pledges, *"Him that cometh to me I will in no wise cast out" (John 6:37).*

Still, in a variety of ways we say, "Send them away." Such is our mindset.

In 2 Kings chapter 4 there is a telling account of a sick young prince who seeks his father's help. His father, the king, orders a servant, *"Carry him to his mother."* "Send him away!" Too many men in our generation echo that when it comes to providing leadership at home: "Leave it to my wife," they say by their silent abdication; or worse, "Leave it to the media to teach them life's important values about morality, language, relationships, and absolutes."

Similarly, thousands call themselves friends of the church, yet do a naked nothing to advance Christ's work through her. Forfeiting opportunities to make a positive difference in Christ's name, they leave others to carry the load. Their cry of non-involvement says, "Don't bother us. Send the needy away!" So, Christ's call to service echoes with every generation, *"The harvest truly is great, but the labourers are few" (Luke 10:2).*

Abortion is not unlike that. In its attempt to quickly escape a difficult situation at the cost of a child's life, to, "Send it away," so to speak, it misses something wonderful Christ *"has in mind."* Imagine how different the history of Europe would have been in this century had Winston Churchill's unmarried mother chosen to abort him.

Suicide, the second highest cause of death among U.S. young people, is the ultimate wishing away. Curt Cobain and Margeaux Hemingway are but two recent well-known examples. Others wish themselves away. David, forsaken by a fair weather friend, wanted out: *"Oh, that I could fly away!"* he exclaims, *(see Psalm 55:6).* Jeremiah's congregation nearly drove him crazy and he wept, *"I wish I could get away from them" (cf. Jeremiah 9:2).* Jonah, called to preach in Nineveh, ran away.

Then, of course, there was that carpenter fellow from Nazareth, Joseph. His fiancee, Mary, was expecting a baby he was certain was not his. Because he was a decent fellow, Joseph *"had in mind"* to put her away quietly rather than embarrass her. It was a nice thought and well intended. But God had in mind something, more accurately, Someone, that would transform history. Joseph's betrothed had been selected to birth God's Savior who would come to Bethlehem's manger and later to Calvary's cross for our sins.

"The people murmured against Moses" (Exodus 15:24). Now, they grumbled against Christ and the potential of five thousand new disciples, of all things. Complaining is nothing new. It is an age old way of running from a problem when we have closed our mind to the possibilities Christ *"already has in mind."*

Philip griped. *"Eight months' wages,"* he said, would not be enough. His was the failed faith of the bottom line that always comes up short. We see it in various forms. People with undersized faith complain and run away when something is not to their liking. They miss what Christ *"has in mind."* How often in church history, I wonder, has revival been forfeited because we evangelicals ran, rather than standing for the message we claim to hold so dear?

Do you remember that famous Clint Eastwood closing line from the movie, Dirty Harry? Clint says to the bad guy, "You can run but you'll never hide." Long before Hollywood scripted it, John Milton's Satan learned that you can run but you cannot hide. There is a principle so woven into the fabric of life that it cannot be separated: No matter where you run you always take yourself with you:

> *"Infinite woe and infinite despair:*
> *Which way I fly is hell; myself am hell!"*

Even Satan realizes we run most often from ourselves and blame it on others. David and Jeremiah stayed. Jonah finally turned and went to Nineveh. Churchill was born, and the world has seen at least something of what God, *"Already had in mind."* Most important of all, Joseph stood by Mary, who had her baby and the world can never be the same again.

The Things Christ Had in Mind!

I like Andrew. He was different from the other disciples. Of all the disciples, he is my favorite, because Andrew is a bringer. I aspire to be a bringer. Andrew brought his brother Peter to Jesus. I'm quite certain that when he did that, Andrew had no idea Christ would look behind Peter's rough exterior and see not only a Galilaean fisherman but one who had in him the strong foundation which would serve as an example for later church development. That is how Christ is. He sees not only the actualities in us, He also sees the possibilities. Bringers discover the amazing miracles that Christ *"already has in mind."*

Now, while the rest complain about the high cost of groceries, Andrew brings a wee boy with a lunch. It was not much. In his own way Andrew says, "It ain't much, but it's all I got." All he could find was all Christ needed. Five barley loaves and two small fishes were the seeds of this great miracle.

I would rather bring than complain any day, wouldn't you? Last week an executive in one of the high rise buildings near our church brought her troubled secretary to

120

our midweek Tuesday Noon Boost service. The secretary heard the message and realized her need to receive Christ. She asked the Lord to come into her life and take control. Resolving to put some old anger behind her once and for all, she relinquished some kingdoms in her heart that she was previously determined to hold. The changes in her life, already remarkable, have taken great courage. It is exciting to witness the progress she is making. Who knows all that Christ *"already has in mind"* for her? So far, He alone does.

Once someone came to Michelangelo chipping away with his chisel at a huge shapeless piece of rock. He asked the sculptor what he was doing. "I am releasing the angel imprisoned inside this marble," he answered. Christ is the only one who can see the hidden greatness inside every one of us, and in every one we bring to Him. How many have you brought to Jesus?

The disciples discovered that Christ always has a positive, constructive plan in mind. Their ideas, on the other hand, were divisive: "Get rid of them," they chorused when they saw that hungry crowd five thousand strong. Had the Lord followed their advice, this miracle would never have happened. The church's missionary march would have ended on a Galilean hillside. We would not have heard the gospel.

In opposition to that, Christ's way says, "Work with me and the bad always gets better." Bring Him all you have, and He multiplies it. That is how Christ's kingdom grows; and we grow. *"I am the vine, ye are the branches: He that abideth in me, and I in him, the same bringeth forth much fruit"* (John 15:5). Don't you know that as Philip watched that boy's lunch multiply, and as he helped pick up the leftovers, he resolved never to worry about money again!

Does some situation in your life seem hopeless? Have you considered, *"The things Christ has in mind?"*

How to Discover What Christ Has in Mind

The four gospel accounts present three vital life principles for discovering what Christ has in mind for us. Philip and the others missed them that day. Andrew did not.

Vital Principle #1 - Believe in God!

Believe in God who made you, and in His Son Christ Jesus. Believe that He exists. Believe who He is; and in what He has done for you. Believe He loves you, for He always does and always will. Act as though you really believe this even when you are tempted to doubt it. Remember His great salvation, provided with you in mind. He died thinking about you. Every time you feel like running away, or wonder if a situation is impossible, remember Christ, *"Already has in mind what he is going to do."*

Vital Principle #2 - Believe in Yourself!

Believe in yourself; not in some self-centered, humanistic way but in the spiritual, theological way Christ believes in you. You are a person made in His image. Away back long ago at Calvary, Christ saw something in you that was worth dying to save. Believe that. *"All things are possible to him that believeth,"* He says *(Mark 9:23).* By God's grace, we can do anything we need to do. You were born to live with faith. *"Everything is possible!"* Jesus says there are no impossibilities! Are there difficulties? Yes. Hardships? Occasionally. Tough times? Sometimes. But, always these things represent opportunities in disguise.

Vital Principle #3 - Believe in Your Future!

Believe in your future. A miracle often awaits you just around the corner when a challenge seems insurmountable. *"For I know the thoughts that I think toward you, saith the LORD, thoughts of peace, and not of evil, to give you an expected end" (Jeremiah 29:11).*

Christ has in mind to save you from your sins and from your situations, and bless your life in ways you have not yet dreamed. *"For the Son of man is come to seek and to save that which was lost" (Luke 19:10).* It was what God had in mind at the incarnation, and what His Son, Christ, had in mind when He took your place on the cross at Calvary.

Wherever you are today, or wherever you find yourself tomorrow, remember this: Christ *"already has in mind what he is going to do"* with you and for you, and it is all good. Stay close to Him and you shall soon declare with David's ultimate certainty, *"Surely goodness and mercy shall follow me all the days of my life: and I will dwell in the house of the LORD for ever" (Psalm 23:6).*

The difficult moments along life's way are merely testing places. John records Christ's motivation: *"He asked this only to test Philip, for he already had in mind what he was going to do."* When we believe in Him, in ourselves, and in our future with Him, we always discover the wonderful things He *"already has in mind."*

Christianity Lite

Have ye received the Holy Ghost since ye believed?
And they said unto him, We have not so much as
heard whether there be any Holy Ghost.

–ACTS 19:2

*H*ave you noticed our grow-
ing national fascination with the lite, that is, L-I-T-E? We have
become a nation of lite lovers. A host of lite products claim to
help us eat more but weigh less. Paul was thinking about
something we might call Christianity lite when he posed a
penetrating question to some elders from Ephesus: *"Have ye
received the Holy Ghost since ye believed? And they said unto
him, We have not so much as heard whether there be any Holy
Ghost."* Lite food is food without fat. Christianity lite is faith
with no fiber. It is a lightweight, impotent version of the gospel, that allows itself to be rattled by externals. It loses sleep
over little things that are ultimately of little consequence. In
adversity it forgets that God is on the throne. *"Have ye received the Holy Ghost since ye believed?"*

Who Is the Holy Spirit?

First, I must tell you that there is nothing mystical about Him. Receiving the Holy Spirit and allowing Him control of your life is not some "hokey" experience for only a select group of super-Christians. The same Paul who questions these Ephesians, writes to the Romans that the Holy Spirit is for all Christians: *"If any man have not the Spirit of Christ, he is none of his" (Romans 8:9)*. Receiving the Holy Spirit is for you.

The Holy Spirit is the Trinity's Third Person who reigns in partnership with God the Father and God the Son. The Bible speaks of God the Father at creation; God the Son dying on our cross. In this text, Paul speaks about the Holy Spirit. The Holy Spirit, is the energizing power of God who is working in and through believers in every generation.

The Bible describes one God who presents Himself three ways to us. Some people find the idea of God being one and three at the same time a bit hard to grasp. So, let me try to illustrate it: My granddaughters, Hannah and Cameron, love to play a game they call, "ride horsey," which means I crawl around on all fours carrying them on my back. When I do that, they delightedly call me, "Horsey Papa!" Not long ago on television Hannah saw me in my preaching robe and exclaimed, "Look! Papa in his church dress!" Occasionally, the two of them find me catching a nap. When that happens they say, "Papa asleep." How many Papas do Hannah and Cameron have? Ask them and they will tell you they have only one. Yet, Papa has appeared to them in three rather distinctive roles; a "horsey Papa," a "church dress Papa," and a "sleeping Papa." So, also, God is Father, Son, and Holy Spirit. He is one God in three roles.

Why It Is Important to Receive the Holy Spirit

"Have ye received the Holy Ghost since ye believed? And they said unto him, We have not so much as heard whether

there be any Holy Ghost." Why is it important to receive the Holy Spirit?

It is important first, because the Holy Spirit comforts us. There are times in your life and mine when there is no true comfort without Him. You stand at the grave with a broken heart. Nothing anyone can say can ease that moment. Some of you have experienced, or are experiencing, other hurts such as divorce, corporate cut-backs, and relationship struggles. Each of these experiences brings its own unique pain. Who can ease it? Only God the Holy Spirit.

Second, it is important to receive the Holy Spirit because He converts. If you are like me, you grew up in the church and you heard the gospel faithfully preached many times. One day the gospel suddenly made sense to you in a way that you had never experienced before, even though you had heard the story many times. Suddenly, the preacher's invitation seemed very personal, as though addressed just to you. That was your special moment with Christ. You knew it was different. In response, you opened your heart to Jesus. You admitted you were a sinner and asked Him to forgive you and to come and live in your heart. What made that day different? It was that God the Holy Spirit, the Divine Converter, made the message of the cross come alive for you.

Third, it is important to receive the Holy Spirit because He guides. You face a hard decision in family or business. You pray asking for wisdom and direction, and make a choice. Perhaps still uncertain, you move ahead on the strength of it. Later you look back and see that everything turned out right. Yet, you know that the decision was not yours alone. God the Holy Spirit guides and makes the way clear for us, often moving in realms we have not yet realized.

Fourth, it is important to receive the Holy Spirit because He brings joy. I love humor. There is a whole bookshelf in my library filled with books of jokes and humorous stories. Now, when I speak of joy I need you to hear that joy is eternally different from humor. *"The fruit of the Spirit is...joy,"* Paul writes to the Galatians *(Galatians 5:22).* Real joy is knowing when you get up in the morning that you can make a positive difference in the universe. God is on your side and will help you in the energizing power of His Spirit to do something wonderful for Him. There is joy at the center of your life because, no matter what happens, you have wonderful, over-riding confidence that the Holy Spirit is in control.

Fifth, it is important to receive the Holy Spirit because He empowers us to fulfill Christ's Great Commission. *"Ye shall receive power, after that the Holy Ghost is come upon you: and ye shall be witnesses unto me both in Jerusalem, and in all Judaea, and in Samaria, and unto the uttermost part of the earth" (Acts 1:8).* God has important work for each of us to do. This promise from the resurrected Jesus promises power to tell what He has done for us so that others may give their lives to Him also.

Did You Receive the Holy Spirit when You Believed?

The question Paul asked the Ephesian elders is just as pertinent for us as for them: Are you living in the full orbed power of new life in Jesus Christ? If not, now is the time to give God the Holy Spirit absolute authority over your life. When you do, He will come into you, and you will go out with Him, and life will be new and better. Who says so? God's only begotten Son, Jesus Christ, the Lord of the cross, that is who.

Receiving the Holy Spirit means opening your life to God's best for you. The good news of the gospel is that the Holy Spirit is willing to come into your life today. If you have not received Him do not allow this moment to pass you by. This is your special moment with Christ. You have heard about the Holy Spirit, now go forward in His power and tell someone about God's love in Jesus Christ.

17

So Long Mediocrity! Hello Enthusiasm!

They entered into a covenant to seek the LORD
God of their fathers with all their heart and
with all their soul.

−2 CHRONICLES 15:12

*T*he prophet Azariah presented positive life principles to Asa, one of Judah's best kings, who lived about three thousand years ago. Azariah's message is still active, powerful and at work in our world. It is as fresh today as it was the day Azariah delivered it for the very first

129

time: Those who seek God always find Him. Those who abandon Him, and His covenant code of conduct, abandon themselves to destruction. For God's ancient people, it was a time of choice, a day of destiny. They had to reject all their old idols and renew their commitment to Jehovah. Otherwise they would reject Jehovah. It could not be God and the idols.

The same rule is true today: It cannot be God and the old life. It must be God or the idols; God or the old life. After nearly a quarter century as a pastor, I have seen this repeatedly. To the extent we give ourselves to God, we will, to the same measure, experience God's blessings on ourselves and our children. *"They entered into a covenant to seek the LORD God of their fathers with all their heart and with all their soul."*

So Long Mediocrity! Hello Enthusiasm!

This text provides another opportunity for us to renew our commitment to Christ; to say, "So long mediocrity!" It allows us to examine anew our own level of commitment to, and enthusiasm for, the blessings we enjoy in Christ.

There is an inescapable, inviolate, spiritual principle behind these words that will always be true: To the extent that we commit our life, will, energy, talents, and resources to God's work; we shall to that degree experience His bounties. The enthusiasm we offer God will be reflected back and multiplied to us. This is a life principle emphasized in both testaments of the Bible: *"Cast thy bread upon the waters: for thou shalt find it after many days"* (Ecclesiastes 11:1). *"Give, and it shall be given unto you; good measure, pressed down, and shaken together, and running over, shall men give into your bosom. For with the same measure that ye mete withal it shall be measured to you again"* (Luke 6:38). The level of enthusiasm we bring to life will be reciprocated in the degree of satisfaction we will receive from it.

On Arturo Toscanini's 80th birthday a friend asked his son, Walter, what the famous conductor considered his most fulfilling achievement. The inquirer expected to hear about some honor conferred by a leading university, or a title from his government, of applause after conducting a great orchestra through a musical masterpiece. Walter Toscanini knew his father better than that. "Dad's most fulfilling achievement is whatever he happens to be doing at the moment; whether it is conducting a symphony or peeling an orange." Enthusiasm! Toscanini had learned that the amount of passion we possess determines how happy, successful and fulfilled we are in life.

En-thus-iasm!

The word enthusiasm is derived from two Greek words, *en* and *Theos* which, taken together, mean, "In God" or "God within." We could say, without stretching the truth, that the word enthusiasm in its truest sense means being full of God. To be enthusiastic is to allow the spark of God's Spirit to ignite your spirit.

To be a Christian is to be, above all else, enthusiastic, or full of God. It means to gain a new exciting upward thinking life perspective. The most enthusiastically passionate person who ever lived was Jesus Christ our Lord. It took incredible gusto for the Lord of heaven to enter the mainstream of human history. It took a level of enthusiasm unequaled in history for God's Son, Jesus, to go through, as the hymn says, "Childhood, manhood, age and death." Only passionate love could have drawn Him to death—especially a death that He did not deserve on a disgraceful Roman cross. It took exuberant imagination to transform that ugly cross into a thing so attractive people will pay Tiffany's good money to purchase one to wear on their neck. You have never heard of Tiffany's gold-plating a hangman's rope, or an electric chair, have you?

Yet, in the Graeco-Roman world the cross was in every way on the level of those two instruments of shameful death. Think about that when depression knocks on your door, or when you are exasperated over something of no great consequence.

God is so enthusiastic about you, and about the gifts He has placed within you, that He sacrificed His only begotten Son to a death on a cross like that to redeem you!

When you watch the cheerleaders at ball games recognize that you too have a cheerleader. His name is Jesus Christ. Jesus was on fire with enthusiasm for the Father's glory, and for the love of us, when He came to live among us. Every time Jesus sees us win against life's challenges He yells, "Yes!" with gusto. He is our best cheerleader.

Five Steps to Life at a New Level!

The world we live in has seen enough of lukewarm Christianity. It is looking for people like you and me to demonstrate that we really believe the message about who Jesus is and what He means to us. There are people all around us who yearn to see faith in Jesus demonstrated on a higher plane than they usually see. Frankly, some of them are unconverted because the type of Christianity they have witnessed presents a picture of life and relationships no different from the world they live in. Strange as it may seem, the unconverted, unregenerate world expects more from those who profess to be disciples of Jesus.

Here are five vital life principles that will guide us as we enter *"into a covenant to seek the LORD God of [our] fathers with all [our] heart and with all [our] soul."* I call them, "Five steps to life at a new level!"

Step 1: Greet Each Day as God's Gift to You!

Greet each new day as a gift from God. Determine that what you make of it will be your gift to God. Practice and personalize Psalm 118:24. Begin today and from here on early each morning repeat to yourself, *"This is the day which the LORD hath made; [I] will rejoice and be glad in it."* I have learned that leaving myself "Post It" reminders of this wonderful verse in the places I frequent is an excellent way of calling me back to its power. I commend that idea to you trusting you will find that power too. Stick one in your desk drawer, another on your mirror, and one more on your car speedometer. Attach one on your telephone until enthusiasm becomes your way of life as a Christian. Live each day to the hilt with your heart pursuing the heart of Christ.

Step 2: Make Christ Your Model!

Make Christ your model in all things. *"Follow his steps"* *(1 Peter 2:21).* In making decisions, or when presented with opportunities, ask yourself, "What would Jesus do in my place?" Then do it with devotion!

One old fellow asked for his Christian testimony replied, "Well, I'm not much for religion and some might say that I'm not making much progress, but I'm established." He thought that line was pretty cute and relished every opportunity to repeat it with a chuckle of laughter.

The next winter he gathered a wheelbarrow full of logs. On the way back to the house, the wheelbarrow wheel sank to the axle in mud. No matter how hard he tried, it would not come free. Finally, as he stood scratching his head in exasperation, a friendly neighbor observed the old fellow's predicament. Offering to lend a helping hand, the neighbor could not resist the temptation to greet the old man with his oft-repeated testimony: "Well, brother, you're not making much progress, but you are certainly established!"

Jesus Christ never calls us merely to be established. To be established is to be stuck, unproductive, ordinary, bogged down. To be established is to live life in a rut but to be in Christ is to live life on an exciting new level.

Step 3: Make the Bible Your Instruction Book!

Make God's book, the Bible, your instruction book for life. *"Wherewithal shall a young man cleanse his way? by taking heed thereto according to thy word" (Psalm 119:9).* Paul, the scholarly apostle, reminds Timothy, the novice preacher, *"All scripture is given by inspiration of God, and is profitable for doctrine, for reproof, for correction, for instruction in righteousness: That the man of God may be perfect, throughly furnished unto all good works" (2 Timothy 3:16, 17).*

Our society is drowning in an ocean of negativism and thought pollution. How can we stay upbeat and be a positive influence for others? Only by turning to a source of strength more powerful than our own. Find a Bible version you can read easily—there are many wonderful new translations—and make it your daily companion. Read it systematically and ask God to help you do what it says. Ask God to help you see the relevance of its message to your life each day and He will.

Step 4: Pray Expectantly Every Day!

Bathe your life in prayer each day. Speak to God as you would to a respected and trustworthy friend. Expect Him to answer. Having prayed, be silent and allow God to speak to you as you reflect on the things you have read in His word. *"Be careful for nothing; but in every thing by prayer and supplication with thanksgiving let your requests be made known unto God. And the peace of God, which passeth all understanding, shall keep your hearts and minds through Christ Jesus" (Philippians 4:6,7).* Come with enthusiasm and remember that God answers our prayers with three words: "Yes. No. Later."

Step 5: Accentuate the Positive –
Demonstrate the Difference!

Earnestly seek out the positive and avoid the negative as much as possible. *"Finally, brethren, whatsoever things are true, whatsoever things are honest, whatsoever things are just, whatsoever things are pure, whatsoever things are lovely, whatsoever things are of good report; if there be any virtue, and if there be any praise, think on these things" (Philippians 4:8).* Feed your mind faith thoughts. When you face a difficult or negative issue or person, ask yourself two questions. First, "Can God do something to turn this problem, or this person, around?" The answer will always be positive. Your second question should be, "What can I do to be God's instrument in helping effect that positive transformation?"

Ask God to make you a bearer of good tidings. The word, "Gospel," comes from the Greek root meaning, "good news." Intentionally design your interactions with non-Christians to be as positive and constructive as possible. Living this way allows others to witness the amazing difference Christ in love is making in you.

"And they entered into a covenant to seek the LORD God of their fathers with all their heart and with all their soul...And they sware unto the LORD with a loud voice, and with shouting." You can too! Why not now?